JIM SMOKE

THOMAS NELSON PUBLISHERS
Nashville • Atlanta • London • Vancouver

Copyright © 1995 by Jim Smoke

Published in Nashville, Tennessee, by Thomas Nelson, Inc., Publishers, and distributed in Canada by Word Communications, Ltd., Richmond, British Columbia.

Library of Congress Cataloging-in-Publication Data

Smoke, Jim.
    Moving forward : finding hope and peace in the midst of divorce / Jim Smoke.
      p.   cm.
    ISBN 0-8407-3382-8 (trade pbk.)
    1. Divorced people—Prayer -books and devotions—English. 2. Divorce—Religious aspects—Christianity. I. Title.
BV4596.D58S56 1995
242'.646—dc20   94-37273
                                            CIP

Printed in the United States of America.

1 2 3 4 5 6 — 00 99 98 97 96 95

ACKNOWLEDGMENTS

To all the divorced men and women who have taught me all I know over the past twenty years.

To my wife, Carol, for critiquing, proofing, and typing this manuscript.

To my literary agents at Alive Communications for making good things happen.

To the kind people at Thomas Nelson Publishers who can team with an author to give birth and life to a book and help put strong wings on weary hearts in today's world.

INTRODUCTION

It has been almost twenty years since I stood before thirty men and women in my first divorce recovery workshop in southern California. I had serious doubts that night that I could alleviate any of the pain they carried and give them a few rays of hope by the end of the five-week workshop. A somber mood hung like a dense fog over this band of strugglers as they realized divorce meant the death of a relationship with their spouse, but they had to keep on living. I sensed that many in that room would have rather chosen their own death than walk the rugged road of personal recovery through divorce country.

After hundreds of workshops and thousands of hours counseling individuals battered by the divorce experience, I now know that healing, hope, happiness, and wholeness can be restored to men and women in our country who have had their dreams destroyed and their families shredded by divorce.

Processing pain and affirming new growth takes time. In his book *A Gift of Hope*, author Robert Veninga says, "Human pain does not let go of its grip at one point in time. . . . There is a season of sadness, a season of anger, a season of tranquility, a season of hope. But seasons do not follow one another in a lockstep manner. . . . The winters and springs of one's life are all jumbled together in a puzzling array . . . but when one affirms that the spring thaw will arrive, the winter winds seem to lose some of their punch."

This devotional guide is written with the hope that you will take each day as it unfolds as you journey through divorce country and know that the words of the psalmist are written for you: "The Lord is close to the brokenhearted and saves those who are crushed in spirit" (Ps. 34:18 NIV).

How to survive a divorce

1. When the reality of divorce hits you, stop long enough to commit your entire situation to God through prayer, and ask Him to provide you with help, guidance, and emotional support.

2. Call your best friends and ask them for their prayers and emotional support.

3. Stay in touch with your feelings and share them with people you can trust.

4. Don't spiritualize your situation. You may have to live out a bad decision that someone else has made.

5. Don't panic! Remember, no matter what happens, God is still in charge.

6. Contact an attorney to find out about your legal grounds.

7. Make a list of all your fears. Then make a list of all your resources.

8. Pull as many members of your family around you as you can. Ask them for their love and support.

9. Seek out a divorce support group in your community. These are often held in churches and community colleges. Buy a copy of *Growing Through Divorce* and read it many times.

10. Remember, healing takes time. There is no quick fix for a divorce.

Living with rejection

The words "I don't love you anymore" stung Ralph's ears. Even now, months after their divorce was final, Ralph is still feeling the pangs of his wife's rejection.

Close to 70 percent of all men and women in divorce recovery workshops have been left for someone else. Whether you have been married one year or thirty-one years, the pain of rejection is perhaps the most difficult feeling to process and work through.

For most of us, rejection starts early in life. We didn't get the highest grade; we were not chosen for the school play or the sports team; our parents did not treat us as well as a brother or sister; or someone we loved did not return that love to us.

All human relationships involve the delicate balance of acceptance and rejection. When we finally marry someone who loves and accepts us, we breathe a sigh of relief knowing that we are very special to one other person on the planet.

The words "I don't love you anymore" or "I never really loved you" or "I love someone else" will put anyone on a collision course with rejection. Our human nature shouts, "If someone I felt loved me rejects me, then no one will ever love me again!"

When you are rejected by someone, focus on these two powerful thoughts: First, say out loud, "I am still God's unique, unrepeatable miracle, and your rejection of me will be *your* loss." Second, focus on today's verse and the strength God can bring into your life. The Lord is your rock and your fortress and deliverer. God is your strength, shield, salvation, and stronghold. What a promise! Human rejection is an unavoidable reality for everyone, but God's permanent, unconditional acceptance of us is a guarantee!

The LORD is my rock and my fortress and my deliverer; My God, my strength, in whom I will trust; My shield and the horn of my salvation, my stronghold.
—Psalm 18:2
NKJV

God, today I will rejoice in Your deliverance of me and in Your acceptance of me as a unique, lovingly designed miracle!

The shock of the unexpected

Sharon had no idea that John was unhappy. She knew that she and John weren't talking much lately, and they were fighting more than usual, but she thought everything would work out eventually. When John told her that he wanted a divorce she was shocked.

For I, the LORD your God, will hold your right hand, saying to you, "Fear not, I will help you."
—*Isaiah 41:13 NKJV*

Like Sharon, about half the people I counsel for divorce never expected to go through a divorce. They often admit to some turbulent times in their marriage, but they thought they had a normal, happy, average marriage until the spouse unexpectedly announced that he or she was leaving and filing for divorce.

The shock of divorce has a way of reducing a normal, healthy, functioning individual to a state of numbness. Even when well-meaning friends try to rouse us from our stupor, we cling to our suspended state, hoping that we are just having a bad dream, and when we awaken everything will be back to normal.

Shock can be a protective armor from the hurt and pain of the moment. Refusing to come out of it can be a denial of the reality that your life must go on without your spouse.

Sharon, like most people in divorce recovery, and perhaps like you, will experience three processes before moving forward with her life: shock, recovery, and growth. The key to getting on with life is to shorten the shock stage and begin to focus on recovery and growth. You must refuse to stay immobilized because you know it will short-circuit your growth. Reach out to those who can help you today and allow God to imprint today's verse on your heart and soul.

God, my divorce is not just a bad dream. I need You to help me overcome this state of shock I am in. Thank You for Your promise to be with me and help me face the future without fear.

The silent questions of your heart

I had just started another six-week divorce recovery workshop in a nearby church. I made all the preliminary announcements and was ready to plunge into the content of the evening. Wanting to make sure that everyone understood my instructions, I asked if there were any questions. It was deathly quiet. No hands were raised, and no questions were asked—out loud. But as my eyes met theirs, I knew the people in that room had hundreds of questions. They were the silent questions that all of us have in times of great pain. "Will I survive this experience?" "How will I survive?" "If I do survive, what kind of shape will I be in?" "Does anyone care enough to help me survive?" "How long will I feel this numbing pain?" "What will happen if I don't survive?"

Unanswered questions usually send our fear levels soaring, and we convince ourselves that there are no answers and that we will surely wither and die in the midst of our crises.

The hope of finding answers to our questions can come cloaked in the form of a fellow struggler who once stood where we now stand. That person's affirmation and encouragement can release a new energy in us that turns our questions from fears to challenges. I believe that God sends people into our lives when we really need them. Are you willing to be open and receptive to the person God might be bringing into your life today? Some of us are so wrapped up in our questions that we miss the people who can show us where the answers are.

May our Lord Jesus Christ himself and God our Father, who has loved us and given us everlasting comfort and hope which we don't deserve, comfort your hearts with all comfort, and help you in every good thing you say and do.
—2 Thessalonians 2:16–17 TLB

God, help me to share my silent questions with You today and then to listen for Your answers.

Forget the past, there's no future in it!

Janet was angry at herself. As she fussed and fumed, she summed up her feelings by saying, "If I'd only married someone else, I wouldn't be in this mess now." Her friends all nodded in agreement as they walked out the door and into the night.

I have heard Janet's statement a thousand times. There are two other lines that follow it: "What if . . . ?" and "I can do it!" We call this talk the divorce recovery syndrome. It usually wakes you up in the middle of the night and prevents you from going back to sleep.

The first statement is prompted by a feeling of regret. The second is prompted by fear, and the third by hope. All three bounce around in your head as you try to sort through your feelings during divorce.

It is easy to lapse into yesterday, worry about tomorrow, and do very little with today. All you can do about yesterday is learn from it. All you can do about tomorrow is plan for it. All you can do about today is live it to its fullest, and tell yourself over and over, "I can do it."

Our verse today comes from the heart of the apostle Paul. He knew what he was talking about because he had a past worth forgetting. He put his own life in perspective by emphasizing the importance of moving forward. He lived in this world but had the next world as his dream and goal. He evaluated the possible prizes and rewards in this life only in light of the Christian's greater reward in the next.

Yesterday is history. Tomorrow is a promise. Where are you living today?

But one thing I do, forgetting those things which are behind and reaching forward to those things which are ahead, I press toward the goal for the prize of the upward call of God in Christ Jesus.
—Philippians 3:13–14
NKJV

God, help me to learn from where I have been and to trust You with where I am going in this life. Help me to keep my eye on the real goal.

When your eyes close and your brain stays open

She looked as if she hadn't slept in days, but there she was nodding off in the front row of my workshop. During the break, she came up to me and apologized and informed me that she was dead tired but had not been able to sleep in days. Sound familiar? Your body runs all day, and your brain runs all night.

It happens periodically to all of us in the normal flow of life. It is drastically accentuated when we face a crisis. Fears that are life-sized in the daylight hours become giant-sized at night when we try to sleep. Unresolved issues and questions become obsessions when the sun goes down and our house lights go out. We wonder if we will ever sleep peacefully again.

When this happens to me, I talk to myself. I ask myself if what I am thinking about and worrying about can be resolved in the middle of the night by a body and brain that are out of sync with each other. The answer is always *No!* I ask myself if the problem or struggle will still be there when I wake up in the morning. The answer is *Yes!* A third question I always ask is, "Is God still in charge here?" I believe we lose sleep when we try to do things our way instead of letting God be in charge.

I think you will sleep better tonight if you trust God's promise and reaffirm that He is still in charge while you sleep!

God, quiet my brain when I need rest. Help me to rest in You and give You all my fears.

Reach for the resources

God is our refuge and strength, a very present help in trouble.
—Psalm 46:1 NKJV

When was the last time you said, "Nobody understands me and nobody can help me." Yesterday? Last week? A few minutes ago?

I hear it quite frequently in counseling sessions after people have told me their stories and dismiss the account by throwing up their hands and saying, "I guess it's my problem, and no one can help me."

What we are really doing is denying that help exists and feeling sorry for ourselves. We invite all who listen to us to become involved in our "pity party."

Pity, whether by extraction or expression, is seldom helpful. Divorced people initially spend a lot of time telling divorce war stories in the hope that others will feel sorry for them. I have learned over the years that the first sign of getting well after divorce is when you get tired of telling your story to any and all who will listen. Eventually you might even forget that you are divorced.

Workshops, counselors, books, and support groups comprise a short list of resources that are available in our country today. Pride, pity, and shame often keep both men and women from reaching out for the resources that will help in their healing process. Good recovery usually happens in community. It rarely happens in isolation.

God, I feel like I have no resources. Keep my heart and mind open to the ones I need today.

Undergirding all our human resources is our spiritual source. David strikes a resonant chord in today's verse: "God is our refuge and strength, a very present help in trouble."

Will you reach out today and risk asking for the help you need from other people and from God?

Can you trust God with your future?

New foundations are often set in the ashes of experience! We try to learn everything we can from what we have done in the past. It is important to write a list of what we learn as we go. That list is often the blueprint for our future.

For I know the plans I have for you, says the Lord. They are plans for good and not for evil, to give you a future and a hope.
—Jeremiah 29:11 TLB

Many of us are fearful to trust God with our future when we feel we trusted Him with our past, and the end result wasn't too good. As a friend of mine says, "God gets blamed for many things He did not cause. Some things are people things, and some things are God things." I think he is right on target.

As Christians, we usually struggle with two sets of plans for our lives: God's plan for us and our plan for ourselves. We usually end up in deep trouble when we superimpose our plan on God's plan.

Living through divorce is seeking God's plan on a daily basis and living it out as it is revealed. Our fearful side will always be close by as we wonder if God really knows what He is doing. Building trust does not happen overnight. Trust means reaching out and taking risks. It is living where others question but where God affirms.

God, I want to trust You, but it is hard. Help me to claim this promise today as my own.

The prophet Jeremiah lived in turbulent times. Everything around him was in flux and doubt. His own existence was uncertain. He needed the assurance of God when He said, "For I know the plans I have for you, says the Lord. They are plans for good and not for evil, to give you a future and a hope."

Are you willing to trust God today?

The problem with waiting is waiting

He has made everything beautiful in its time.
—Ecclesiastes 3:11 NKJV

I hate waiting in lines! I will do anything I can to avoid it. I cannot find any useful way to spend my time while I am standing in a line. I sigh a lot in lines and shift my weight from one foot to the other. I glance at my watch every few seconds and try to convey the overall message to everyone else in line that I am in a hurry and really don't deserve to wait in the line at all. No one seems dramatically affected by my impatience. I am not a good waiter.

There is a lot of waiting for things to happen in life. We wait for paperwork, mechanical work, road work, raises at work, and we wait for things that don't work to start working. Happiness would be having everything in our life work without waiting for it.

Working on myself takes a lot of waiting. There is no way to speed up my emotions, feelings, and struggles. There is no quick fix for betrayal, sorrow, panic, pressure, desperation, or hostility (to name only a few emotions we all deal with at different times).

Many people I know are waiting for a divorce to become final, for property to be sold, for child support to be arranged, and for a new life to begin. I am usually dubbed insane when I tell divorced people it takes two to three years to process all their "stuff." Both external and internal work take time, and individuals only short-circuit their growth when they hurry.

God, I have a hard time waiting on You. Help me to begin to live on Your timetable.

Solomon understood the waiting concept better than you or I. In Ecclesiastes 3:11, he simply states, "He has made everything beautiful in its time." I wonder if Solomon knew my mother. She always said, "Good things come to those who wait."

I need to work harder at getting on God's timetable. How about you?

When the bank runs out of your money

The Toys R Us store is a child's delight and a grandparent's nightmare. My six-year-old grandson and I were there a while back. When it came time to leave (it's never time for a child to leave a toy store), my grandson picked up a rather expensive model and said, "I want this." I looked at the price tag and informed him I didn't have that much money. With his six-year-old mind running at full speed, he looked up at me and said, "Let's go to the bank and get some!"

Simple problem, simple solution. When you need more money, go to the bank.

What happens when you have a mountain of bills to pay, and the bank has run out of "your" money? That happens pretty frequently when you go through a divorce. Economic realities can quickly lead to an economic disaster, and fear can take up permanent residency in your home or apartment.

A divorce is costly, and the carrying charges go on for years, surrounded by the fear of what will happen if there is no job and no money.

God does not call you to live in fear of economic disaster. He wants you to work hard, but He also wants you to trust in His provision when you are in doubt. Today's verse assures you that God will give you everything you *need* "and more, so that there will not only be enough for your own needs, but plenty left over to give joyfully to others."

That's a promise to believe, even when the bank runs out of your money!

God is able to make it up to you by giving you everything you need and more, so that there will not only be enough for your own needs, but plenty left over to give joyfully to others.
—2 Corinthians 9:8 TLB

God, help me to believe this promise today. When I'm down to nothing, help me to believe even more!

What can I do for you?

He sat across from me as the appointment began. As I often do, I opened the conversation by asking the question, "How can I help you?" His response was, "I don't know if you can, but I sure hope you can."

Many conversations in the business world begin with the question, "What can I do for you?" There are times in my work when I am fearful of asking the question because the response that follows may make tremendous demands on me and my time. And I may not be able to fulfill those demands.

People in pain have great needs that often cannot be met in simple and quick ways or with a written "how-to" list. You may find yourself in that position today as you read these words. You may have shared your needs with someone only to have them ignored or not treated seriously. You may have decided to build your protective wall a little higher so that no one can see you or your needs.

Luke 18:35–43 tells the story of how Jesus healed a blind beggar. As Jesus was approaching Jericho, the blind beggar cried out to Him for mercy. Jesus looked at the eyes that could not look back at Him and asked, "What do you want me to do for you?" Strange question when the answer was obvious. The man could have responded by asking for money, eye surgery, better living conditions, or a Seeing Eye dog. But he didn't. He went straight to the heart of his need and said, "I want to see." And Jesus restored his sight. A miraculous healing triggered by a simple question: "What can I do for you?"

God, I commit to You today what I have written down. Help me to trust You for the answers.

What do you need to ask Jesus to do for you today? Take a minute right now and ask Him in prayer. Then write out what you requested on a card, and keep it handy to remind you.

Finding family

My father was killed in an auto accident when I was six months old. Several years later my mother remarried, and a couple of years later, my sister was born. We were a blended family before the term ever became popular. We all got along just fine, but I lived with one small problem: I carried the family name of my biological father, whereas my sister carried my stepfather's family name. For all my growing-up years, I carried the "oddball" name in my family, and I still do. There were many times I wished my mother and stepfather had changed my last name to theirs.

Names often change after divorce. Families definitely change after divorce. Multiple divorces happen so frequently that family members need a directory to know where and to whom they belong.

When our primary families are destroyed, we reach out to build extended families. Our need to belong to someone, somewhere, never ends. Meaningful relationships authenticate our existence. Without them, our life would have little meaning.

Living through divorce means shoring up family connections that remain and starting new ones that can fill the void. During the rebuilding process, it is important to know that, along with your need for an earthly family connection, you can forever belong to God's family. You can find a deep sense of security in today's scripture promise. Belonging to God's family will give you an extended family so large, it can never be counted.

Earthly families come together and split apart. God's family is permanent. You can live today with the confidence of knowing you belong to His family.

For his Holy Spirit speaks to us deep in our hearts, and tells us that we really are God's children.
—Romans 8:16 TLB

God, I sometimes feel a deep sense of loss in my family. Help me to feel loved and secure in Your family.

When do I get to celebrate?

It came in the morning mail. As I opened the envelope, I saw it was an invitation to a party. The invitation read, "You are invited to my 'coming out of the end of my tunnel' party." It was from a woman who had gone through one of my workshops eighteen months before. As I wrote the date on my calendar, I wondered how many of us go through the deep, dark tunnels of struggle in life and are wise enough to celebrate those moments when we once again walk into the light.

There are too few celebrations in most of our lives. Birthdays, anniversaries, weddings, and holidays mark our infrequent galas in life. In the remaining days of the year, we do battle with the dragons and demons of our existence.

On the last evening of our six-week divorce recovery workshops, we have a party. People eat food, laugh, hang around, and generally enjoy themselves until we are kicked out of the room. It is a moment of reprieve that says, "Divorce recovery is hard work, but I can celebrate my growth thus far."

The wisest man who ever lived, King Solomon, talked about life as being lived in seasons. He authenticated our humanity by acknowledging the expression of our feelings when he said, "A time to weep, and a time to laugh; a time to mourn, and a time to dance."

Divorce is the death of a relationship, and weeping and mourning mark the end of that relationship. To weep and mourn forever would be a deterrent to our growth. When it is time to move on, we can mark that decision by a celebration, laughing and dancing with those who have spent some time in the tunnel with us. How do you plan to mark your transition from darkness to light?

Mountains to climb

In the summer of 1971, I set out to climb Mount Whitney with a group of teenagers. Our sole ambition was to reach the top and be able to say we had climbed the highest mountain in the lower forty-eight states.

As we reached the thin air and switchbacks of Mount Whitney, I thought of two things: the popular song "Climb Every Mountain" and the idea of turning around and going home. What started out as a dream climb for our group soon became a sick escapade for crazy teenagers. The thinner the air became, the thinner our numbers became. Sadly, only a few of our group got to the top. The rest of us said, "Wait till next summer!"

We all have goals and dreams. They appear easier to accomplish when we are young. As the decades slip by, some of our dreams are dashed on the rocks of reality, while others are dimmed by life's unplanned interruptions. Living happily ever after is no longer a guarantee tied to a wedding ceremony and a gold wedding band, as more than a million and a quarter Americans discover every year.

When dreams die, it is easy to become cynical and live defensively. We want to blame others for destroying our dreams. Repressed anger and a vengeful spirit sap our energies and keep us from dreaming new dreams and climbing new mountains.

Divorce is a mountain to climb. It will take all your energy, wisdom, and optimism to make that climb. Some days you will be climbing and making progress, while other days it will seem that you are sliding back down the mountain.

I believe it takes love and faith to climb mountains in divorce country. They will always be there, and that's the challenge.

And though I have all faith, so that I could remove mountains, but have not love, I am nothing.
—1 Corinthians 13:2 NKJV

God, give me mountain climbing faith that is supported by Your love for me today.

14

Will I ever be happy again?

I have a sign on my desk that says, *God is up to something!* People who notice it often ask me what I think God is up to. My patented response is, "A million different things in a million different lives." The problem is that God doesn't tell us in advance exactly what He is going to do. We can only live in anticipation of His surprises. That's what makes life exciting. You never quite know what will happen when you give your life to God one day at a time. He can fill it with challenges that stretch you or serendipitous discoveries that excite you.

Divorce makes you wonder what God is really up to in your life. Happiness can seem in short supply when challenges are abundant. You may even begin to doubt the words the apostle Paul wrote to the early church at Philippi: "Being confident of this very thing, that He who has begun a good work in you will complete it until the day of Jesus Christ."

God never starts something in your life or mine and then abandons us before His work is complete. When all the problems of divorce pile up in your life, it is easy to wonder if God is still around and if He still loves you and cares about your happiness and your future. There will be some days when all you can do is cling to the promises of God, smile knowingly, set your jaw, and move ahead one step at a time.

Author Basil Pennington, a Cistercian monk, says, "Happiness consists in knowing what we want and then knowing we have it or are on the way to getting it." Do you know today what you want? Does God want the same thing for you? Are you slowly and gently making progress toward your objectives?

Being confident of this very thing, that He who has begun a good work in you will complete it until the day of Jesus Christ.
—Philippians 1:6 NKJV

God, I know You are up to something in my life. Help me to be patient enough to see Your plan revealed.

I'm so lonely I could die!

It was question and answer time in our weekend workshop. I thought I was tossing out some good answers until one person asked, "What do you do when there is no special person there for you at the end of the day and through the weekends?" There was no easy answer to that question.

You may be wondering the same thing right now, and I need to assure you of two things: Everyone experiences loneliness, and there is no easy answer.

Loneliness is brought on by social and emotional isolation from meaningful relationships with others. In divorce, you not only lose your best friend—your spouse—but you may also lose long-standing friends the two of you shared as a couple. You instantly become a small, isolated island that other humans quickly pass by. "Quarantined" may well describe how you feel.

All the books on loneliness that I have read offer the same semi-solution: Get busy with other people, and make new friends. The second half of the prescription tells you to get busy on yourself.

A good starting point is to close your eyes right now and envision God reaching out to you and taking your hand in His. Imagine Him repeating the promise He made in Isaiah 42:6. You can have a friendship with the Creator that will last forever.

Someone said, "Loneliness is a gift that reminds us of our humanity. It is the thing that continually drives us to a relationship with God and our neighbors."

I, the Lord, have called you in righteousness; I will take hold of your hand. I will keep you.
—Isaiah 42:6
NIV

God, I'm struggling with loneliness. Here's my hand. Thank You for Your promise.

Revenge can be hazardous to your health

"I don't want his money! I want revenge!"

I cringed as I listened to this comment. I hear it often. It's a recurrent theme that says, "You hurt me, and now I want to hurt you back." It can start in the attorney's office, transfer to the judge's courtroom, and often conclude with emotional or personal injury to one party or the other.

When someone we once loved, or still do love, hurts us, our human inclination is to hurt that person in return. We want to even the score, retaliate, and let the person know that he or she cannot live unpunished for what has been done.

It takes mental and emotional energy to stay angry and focus on revenge. Revenge is consuming and debilitating to all of us. Revenge is allowing the other person to control us and dominate our thoughts and actions. The battle for revenge is never fought on level ground, and those who feel they can win something end up being permanent losers.

The desire for revenge is human but not Christian. The Bible contains many accounts of people who sought revenge, but it offers strong instructions about dealing with it. In today's scripture, the apostle Paul urges us to give up vengeful thoughts and actions, and replace them with the things that promote love and forgiveness.

I doubt seriously that Paul had divorce in mind when he wrote the words in today's verse, but he certainly included all the emotions people feel in divorce. It defies our realities when we are told to forgive instead of seeking revenge. God's way may not be your way today, but I challenge you to try it, and stop wasting your precious energy trying to even accounts through vengeful acts.

Let all bitterness, wrath, anger, clamor, and evil speaking be put away from you, with all malice. And be kind to one another, tenderhearted, forgiving one another, even as God in Christ forgave you.
—Ephesians 4:31–32 NKJV

God, I have some lessons to learn in forgiveness. Help me to trade revenge for love!

High anxiety

Anxiety and stress sit at opposite ends of the teeter-totter called life. They conspire to keep most of us up in the air permanently. They are as common and accepted as the air we breathe, but they are not our friends. They are enemies and robbers of our peace and joy in life.

"So don't be anxious about tomorrow. God will take care of your tomorrow too. Live one day at a time."
—Matthew 6:34 TLB

The dictionary defines anxiety as a "disturbance of mind regarding some uncertain event; misgiving or worry."

Divorce is an uncertain event. There are no guarantees or happy endings to count on. Questions and feelings, actions and reactions swirl through our life in jumbled array. It is little wonder that many people refer to divorce as "crazy time."

Anxiety and stress will not soon disappear from our lives. In all probability, both will increase and we will need to learn some form of management, or we will be reduced to babbling mounds of humanity.

God understands how we feel and what we face better than we do. He gives us His solutions to our problems. When we employ them, we are better able to keep our lives in balance.

God, don't let my anxieties and fears crowd faith out of my life today or any day.

In the Sermon on the Mount, Jesus urged His listeners not to be anxious about tomorrow. He promised that God would take care of their tomorrows and urged them to live one day at a time.

Much of our anxiety comes from our fears. Our fears are based in the "what if's" of our tomorrows.

Is your focus on today, with the knowledge that God is in charge right now, and He will also be in charge tomorrow? Living one day at a time reduces stress and anxiety in all of us.

Growing strong when feeling weak

She was a single mother of three children. She left for work at 7:00 A.M. five days a week and returned home at 6:00 P.M. Crammed into her evening were cooking dinner, doing laundry, supervising homework, preparing school lunches for the next day, and periodically attending sports events involving her children. Weekends meant more laundry, housecleaning, children's activities, and church activities; every other weekend meant getting the kids packed to visit their father. Add about thirty other maintenance chores, and you have the life of a single parent with primary custody. It is little wonder that this mother's fervent prayer was, "God, give me a strong man with good credit whom I can marry!"

All the time in the lives of most of the single parents I know is consumed with physical and emotional responsibilities. "Tired and worn out" is generally their response to the question, "How are you?"

Finding someone to share the load would be wonderful, but most single parents have to dig in and face each new day knowing that the load is theirs alone.

Finding the strength to carry on comes from getting enough physical rest and tapping into one's spiritual resource. Today's verse from the book of Isaiah offers words of hope to the worn down and wound out.

It may seem strange that growing strong when feeling weak starts with simply waiting on the Lord. You and I can do that today by opening our hands and hearts to God and waiting before Him in silence for His strength to come to us.

But those who wait on the LORD shall renew their strength . . . they shall run and not be weary, they shall walk and not faint.
—Isaiah 40:31 NKJV

God, I'm tired. Give me enough strength to make it through each day. Help me to wait on You.

Scar tissue to star tissue

Scars on the body are plainly visible, but scars on the heart are hidden. Physical wounds heal more quickly than wounds of the heart. Scars on the heart loom as formidable challenges to the healing process of divorce recovery.

"I am the Lord who heals you."
—Exodus 15:26
TLB

Emotional scars are often the result of uncaring actions from the people we care about. The scars can stay with us for a lifetime, but we know that healing is taking place when we quit calling attention to our scars.

When a person is newly divorced, he or she may talk for days on end about the pain and hurt caused by the divorce. I have told many people that they begin to grow and become whole when they quit talking about their divorce every time they get a live audience.

My friend Robert Schuller used to say that people can choose to turn their scars into stars. I believe that he is right. Healing is always a choice for us. Healing takes time, but we must use the time wisely by seeking the help we need from others, as well as ourselves.

God is a part of the healing process also. From Old Testament times to today, God brings healing to each of us. Today's verse contains God's promise to heal us. Ask God today to help you turn your scars into stars.

God, I've got more scars than stars today. By Your power, help me to have more stars than scars.

Going to court

How can a relationship that was tied together so beautifully in a warm and wonderful ceremony in front of friends and family end in the cold, impersonal, drab hearing room at the local courthouse? After ten, twenty, thirty, or forty years? I wondered that when I recently left a divorce hearing.

So we may boldly say: "The LORD is my helper; I will not fear. What can man do to me?"
—Hebrews 13:6
NKJV

You may be wondering the same thing today, and you may be searching in vain for some kind of answer to help you make sense of your postmarital debris.

I have gone to court with many people over the years. I have stared down marble hallways lined with divorce combatants and their attorneys. I have felt tension like electricity in the air and wondered how lives can separate, families can break up, homes can be sold, and property can be divided by the rap of a judge's gavel.

If your venture into the halls of justice is in your past, you can be thankful and file the memories away. If your day in court is yet to come, I want to offer some suggestions from my experience. First, don't go alone. Take a friend or two with you for moral support. Second, invite the Lord to go along with you. The promise in today's verse from Hebrews assures us that the Lord is here to help us, and we have no reason to fear what other people can do to us.

God, go with me to the places that are hard to go to. Fill me with Your strength when I have to be in those places.

Hearings, mediation, conciliation, and depositions are all journeys into the unknown. Even with a good attorney by your side, there is usually a high level of fear over the outcome of any legal process. When you have to go through the unfamiliar, know that the Lord is your helper, and you need not fear what *anyone* can do to you.

Spiritual growth is coming alive

Can you remember the last time you felt fully alive? When you are walking through the valley of pain, it may be hard to focus on such a moment. It is a special experience, an *Aha!* moment, that is usually hard to sum up in words. When it happens, you want to capture it, hug it to yourself, celebrate it, and never let it go.

I have come that they may have life, and that they may have it more abundantly.
—John 10:10 NKJV

This kind of experience is often called a mountain-top experience. For many of us, it appears that the valleys in our lives far outnumber the mountaintops.

John Powell, writing in *Fully Human, Fully Alive,* says there are five things that contribute to one's sense of being fully alive. They are: 1) to accept oneself; 2) to be oneself; 3) to forget oneself in loving; 4) to believe; and 5) to belong. To these five, I would add my own: to care for others and allow them to care for you.

Take a minute right now, and ask yourself if you are doing each of these six steps. If you are in the process of divorce right now or have gone through it in the past eighteen months, you probably will answer *No* more times than *Yes.*

God, I know I'm human. Help me to be fully alive today and to keep rebuilding my life with Your help.

Living through and beyond divorce means rebuilding your life. It means tackling the hard things that will stretch you and pull you out of your hiding place. Yes, you have mountains to climb today. As you prepare to do so, remember that Jesus has come that we all may experience life to its fullest. Get going!

When is it happy hour in your day?

I don't know why they call it happy hour, but it seems that every bar in my town has one. At about five o'clock every day, thousands of office employees race to a local bar to drink alcohol (a known depressant). Many who do not drink alcohol hang around and talk about how bad things are at work and at home. This is a happy hour?

Commit everything you do to the Lord. Trust him to help you do it and he will.
—Psalm 37:5
TLB

Psychology, that great field of study that can tell us why we do the things we do, also tells us that there are three things in life that make people happy: 1) having something to do; 2) having someone to love; and 3) having something to look forward to. I agree that is a good foundation for happiness. We are energized and receive affirmation from creative and meaningful things to do. We need someone in our lives to receive the love and affection that we give, and we need someone to return that love and affection to us. We also need things in our future that excite and challenge us. Right now, I believe half the people in Phoenix, the city in which I live, are looking forward to getting away from the infamous summer heat for a time. The other half has just returned.

God, it's easy to say I love You. Help me to say it to those near me today who need to hear it.

Divorce can do a clean sweep through all three things listed above and leave you with nothing to do, no one to love, and nothing to look forward to. You may decide that your happy hour is when you are asleep and do not have to think about what you no longer have.

Let me suggest that each day you take a few minutes to plan your own happy hour by deciding to do one thing that day that will be fulfilling for you and others: Find one person in your day to say "I love you" to, or plan one small thing each day to look forward to. God's promise to you today from the book of Psalms can help you do that.

Recovery is setting some goals

Are you a goal-oriented person? Do you have some long- and short-range goals in your life that you are consistently working on? Someone once said, "Shoot at nothing, and that is exactly what you will hit." A goal is a target that defines your aim. Most of us sit down on the first day of a new year and write our resolutions that are, in reality, goals. By the end of January, those goals are gathering moss in a corner of our lives.

Goals give direction and purpose to life. They inject meaning into our human existence. They give us a reason to celebrate when we attain them. They are the mileposts that allow us to measure how far we have come and how well we have done.

I once asked a woman in one of my workshops to name her biggest goal. She sighed and said, "Just to keep breathing each day." I have no doubt that her goal was important to her survival. My problem with it was that it was only a maintenance goal. With a maintenance goal you keep up and keep even, but you may never move beyond where you now are.

The apostle Paul wrote about his goal in life: "I press toward the goal for the prize of the upward call of God in Christ Jesus." Even though his goal was far ahead, Paul focused on it daily and moved toward it.

Where do you want to be a year from now? What do you want to be doing career-wise? Where do you want to live geographically? What kind of people do you want as friends? What do you need to begin doing today to reach those goals? Or are you just looking for someone in your life who has a good list of goals that you can blend in with? Setting your own goals is your responsibility. Attaining them will be your celebration!

*I press toward the goal for the prize of the upward call of God in Christ Jesus.
—Philippians 3:14 NKJV*

God, help me to set some goals that will move me ahead in my journey.

How will I survive financially?

A divorce is expensive, both emotionally and financially. Eventually, the emotions subside, but the drastic change in your finances may go on for years. I meet very few men and women who are financially secure after a divorce. Most live on the nervous edge of trying to stretch too few dollars across the chasm of too many bills. Many single parents who are granted child support and alimony in a divorce settlement never see a dime of the money. Millions of dollars remain uncollected each year, and family units are dramatically affected by this unfulfilled commitment.

A lack of money can cause tremendous strain on family members during post-divorce recovery. Children blame the parents, and the custodial parent gets angry at the former spouse and the children. It is difficult to live in a tension-filled home.

Custodial parents need to make all family members aware of their current financial realities and build a plan where all can contribute to the solution. Hoping that you will win the lottery or that a former spouse will fulfill financial responsibilities is not a hope to cling to. Develop your own economic plan, and try to assume financial responsibility for yourself.

As you are doing all you possibly can to be financially responsible, plug into the spiritual reality of God's continuing care for you and your family. Today's scripture speaks to all of us about our needs.

Trust is letting God do what He says He will do in His time. Today is a good day to start doing that.

And my God shall supply all your need according to His riches in glory by Christ Jesus.
—Philippians 4:19
NKJV

God, I trust You to meet my financial needs. Grant me a spirit of peace.

Crisis navigation

My faith and your faith are seldom tested on calm seas. Our faith is tested in stormy situations when there appears to be little relief in sight. Who you and I really are usually emerges in a crisis, great or small. Many people going through divorce have a tendency to throw away whatever faith they had, believing it did not work because it did not prevent the divorce. Others find that the little faith they had was tremendously strengthened through their divorce.

Fulfill my joy by being like-minded, having the same love, being of one accord, of one mind.
—Philippians 2:2
NKJV

One of Paul's most practical letters was written to the church at Philippi. We know it as the epistle of joy, even though Paul most likely wrote this letter during his first Roman imprisonment. Yet, in this crisis situation he talked about rejoicing and sharing his faith. He modeled for early believers what he hoped they would do when their own crises came—rejoice!

I know what you are thinking: "Am I supposed to rejoice in my divorce? You have to be kidding!"

Hold on. I am not saying you should rejoice in the fact that you are getting a divorce. What I am saying is that you can rejoice in the knowledge that God is in charge of this crisis in your life and will guide you through it.

God, I trust You for joy in my misery. Help me to navigate the rapids of divorce.

There are three practical things you can do to navigate your way through the crisis of divorce. First, deepen your relationship with the Lord by focusing on some things that produce personal growth. Second, work at building a strong supportive community of Christian friends around you. Third, reach out and ask for help when you need it.

A crisis is when the unexpected gives you an opportunity to grow. The place of joy and the place of pain are sometimes the same place!

The recovery principle

I have a problem receiving things from others. I am not sure why. I just feel uncomfortable when people give things to me. I feel much better when I am doing the giving. Perhaps giving puts me in control of a situation, and when I am not in control, I get nervous.

I have met scores of people with my problem. I encounter them in my workshops all the time. They sit in a small sharing and support group with their hands folded, legs crossed, faces rather grim, and they add very little to the discussion. They seem to deny anyone the opportunity to help them. If they cannot control the conversation, they remain deadly silent.

Any form of recovery demands openness and vulnerability from everyone. Giving and receiving must be combined to bring healing and hope, no matter what kind of recovery group one is in.

Over the years, I have used many leaders in our divorce support groups. All have been through a divorce themselves and received help from others. Leading a group is their opportunity to give back to others. It often helps them to shift their focus from being self-centered to being others-centered. They have realized that to continue their own recovery, they must give to those who are not as far along as they are.

Are you receiving and giving as you attempt to grow through your divorce? Today's scripture is really a promise that challenges us to take the lead in giving when we might feel we have nothing to give. God's promise is that we will have more given to us than we will know what to do with, if we will be the initiators of the process.

What's the recovery principle? Give, and you shall receive. Receive, and you will give.

"Give, and it will be given to you: good measure, pressed down, shaken together, and running over will be put into your bosom. For with the same measure that you use, it will be measured back to you."
—Luke 6:38
NKJV

God, sometimes it's hard to give when I feel empty. Help me to learn Your principle of giving.

The freedom to fail

I was never good at math. I failed so many times, my teachers finally passed me so that I wouldn't be the only kid in class with a beard. I never planned to fail math; I just couldn't pass. I passed everything else with flying colors, but I will always be a math flunker (who had kind teachers).

"Forgive, and you will be forgiven."
—*Luke 6:37*
NKJV

Failing at one thing does not mean you are a failure at other things. It does not make you a failure in life. Failures can be acknowledged and learned from. Anyone can build upon what he or she learns from failure. Someone has said, "The greatest failure in the world is to learn nothing from failure."

One of the greatest freedoms we have is the freedom to fail. That does not mean we plan to fail. We plan to succeed, but we have the freedom not to succeed.

Divorce is the failure of a relationship between two people. Does a failed marriage mean that you will now be a failure in other areas of your life? Definitely not.

Some divorced people have told me they were the only ones in their families to ever get divorced. Somehow, their families keep reminding them of that and make it tough for them to recover from the experience. Many families would like to freeze those who fail and suspend them in their failure forever.

God, teach me well the lessons of forgiveness, and may those in my life be healed because of it.

Recovery from any failure usually starts by taking a strong dose of the medicine of forgiveness. We fail both humans and God. The doorway to healing is open in both areas when we ask for forgiveness. When we fail God, we ask for His forgiveness and He grants it. When we fail each other, we ask for forgiveness, and relationships are renewed. When we fail ourselves, we have to forgive ourselves by realizing that we are not perfect, but we are worthy of forgiveness.

Today's scripture encourages you to take the initiative in forgiveness. Will you?

The therapy of tears

There seemed to be a terrible incongruity in life when I was growing up. I was told that big boys don't cry, but I noticed that all the girls around me could cry anytime they felt like it. Many years later, I met men who were told the same thing I was told and who have cried only a little, or not at all, in their lives. Crying was depicted as a sign of weakness, and men were supposed to be strong. Women could cry because they were supposed to be weaker than men.

I am still trying to get rid of some of the dumb things I was told as a kid. I have long since learned it is okay for me to cry. But I meet many men and some women who have years of tears dammed up behind emotional walls.

Tears may well be the best expression of our humanity. Tears can bring us closer to one another in a way that words can never do. They are the door opener to what is in our hearts and what is going on inside our heads. Our tears can weld us to each other in an enduring way.

I watch streams of tears flow down the faces of divorcing people. Some are tears of sadness and loss, and others are tears of joy and freedom. The streams are never-ending. Real men and women have the freedom to cry!

Today's scripture acknowledges our tears and assures us that God will one day wipe them away for us. For now, God's gift of tears may be the best therapy in our lives.

And the Lord GOD will wipe away tears from all faces.
—Isaiah 25:8 NKJV

God, I feel as though I have cried enough to fill a river. As my healing comes, may my tears of sadness lessen and my joy increase.

Confronting closure

Bill looked like death warmed over. As we talked, he told me he felt like he had died right along with his marriage.

Many people going through divorce confirm Bill's feeling. Divorce is the death of a relationship. The struggle for most people is how to conduct a fitting memorial service that will bring closure. One of the toughest things I do is to try to convince people to let go of something that no longer exists and get on with their lives.

Divorce is very different in one way from the physical death of a spouse. In divorce, if you have children you still have to deal with the ex-spouse (the person you are trying to "bury") on an ongoing basis. The goal is to detach yourself enough so that you recapture your own personhood.

Detachment that leads to closure is generally a process marked by different steps and acts. There is no guaranteed format that works for everyone. You must find something that will bring closure for you. I have known people who have melted down their wedding rings, locked away their wedding photos, bought new houses or new cars, or found new jobs. All are ways of declaring, "That was then, and this is now!"

All of us need a sense of closure and new beginnings. Joy and sorrow appear to be liberally sprinkled in both. Only by finishing something do we allow ourselves to start something new.

Today's scripture affirms God's love for us by telling us we will not walk alone through relationships and marriages that die. When we struggle with letting go, God is there to help us.

Yea, though I walk through the valley of the shadow of death, I will fear no evil; for You are with me; Your rod and Your staff, they comfort me.
—Psalm 23:4 NKJV

God, it is hard to face the death of anything. Give me the strength to face today, knowing You will comfort me.

Freedom from fear

Fear is something that most of us deal with on a daily basis. Healthy fear acts as a protective device that keeps us from getting hurt and endangering our lives. Unhealthy or destructive fear immobilizes us and deters us from growth and productivity.

Whenever I am afraid, I will trust in You.
—Psalm 56:3 NKJV

There are eight basic fears that most of us encounter: 1) fear of taking risks; 2) fear of failure; 3) fear of what others will think; 4) fear of rejection; 5) fear of inadequacy; 6) fear of failing health; 7) fear of the future; and 8) fear of success.

As you study this list, which fears are most predominant in your life right now, and what control are they exerting in your life? When I present this list to people going through divorce, they often smile and tell me the only one they are not dealing with is the fear of success, and they would trade the entire list for that one any day.

You must identify your fears before you can resolve them. This can be a long and difficult process, and you may need the help of a therapist or a strong, supportive community of caring friends. When your fears are removed, trust enters your life and gives you the confidence that you can move forward in faith, accepting any and all challenges in your daily recovery.

God, I confess my fears to You today and ask that You will divinely apply Your trust to each one.

There will still be times when you have recurring moments of fear. David's words today can help: "Whenever I am afraid, I will trust in You." It is God's desire that we live in faith and trust, and He gives us a sure anchor when we are buffeted by fear.

I need to know what to do

I start my day with a long list of questions. What do I need to get done today? Do I have the time to get it all done? How will I deal with the things I don't want to do today or any day? How will I solve the problems associated with the things I have to do?

If any of you lacks wisdom, let him ask of God, who gives to all liberally and without reproach, and it will be given to him.
—James 1:5 NKJV

Some days I wish I could hire someone who could correctly and wisely answer my questions for me. You may feel the same way. Life has far more questions than answers.

I spend many hours every week counseling with people who come to me with questions that often have no quick or easy answers. Questions such as, "How do I get my former spouse to spend more time with our children?" "How do I deal with a vindictive former spouse, who constantly disrupts my life with threats of abuse?" "Should I stay here or move to another state?" "How do I find work when I have few marketable skills?" "How can I be a good dad when my children live far away from me?" "When will the pain stop?"

Those are only a few of the hundreds of questions I listen to. They are the easier ones. Many have no immediate or even long-term answers. It takes wisdom to ask the right questions and even more wisdom to supply the answers.

God, my biggest question seems to be, "Why me?" I hear You saying, "Trust me." Help me to do that today!

We do not have to face our questions alone. We can ask for guidance from our most objective and caring friends, from a therapist or counselor, and we can ask God for His guidance. I believe it is best to ask God first. Today's verse promises that God will answer our questions and give us wisdom "liberally and without reproach."

Be aware that God takes time to respond to your questions, so don't become impatient and feel He doesn't care. Ask God today to help you find the answers to your questions in life.

Tapping into God's awesome power

She sat in my office and slowly exhausted my supply of Kleenex. Through her tears she told me she once felt like she had some control and power in her life, but because of her divorce all of that had changed, and she now felt totally powerless.

How tremendous is the power available to us who believe in God.
—Ephesians 1:19 JBP

Losing power can be equated with losing control. It is easy to fall into the role of victim when you have no control over anything, and someone else seems to be pulling the strings.

How much power does a person need to be in control of his or her life and destiny? Where do people go when they want real power? How about going to God. How much of God's power is available to us each day? The answer is all of it, including His creative power in forming the world, His continuing power in sustaining the world, and His resurrection power in overcoming the world.

Rebuilding your life after divorce can be a form of resurrection. It is coming back from death—the death of a relationship and a marriage. Resurrection power is the power of a new life, the power to rebuild, renew, or change.

God, some days I feel powerless. Help me to quit grasping for the world's kind of power and tap into Your power to live.

In writing to the Christians at Ephesus, Paul told them two things about God. The first was that His power was tremendous. It was not some puny power but an awesome power that no one else in the universe possessed. Second, Paul wanted every Christian to know that God's power is available to anyone who believes in God.

Knowing that God's power is readily available for us in all situations gives us the strength to face life's daily conflicts and struggles. We need that power to live, to meet frustrations, to make the right decisions, and to make the right changes.

Are you tapping into God's power today? Try it. You may be surprised at the results.

Having feelings is human

It is not easy for me to share my feelings with people I don't know. It is not so much my fear of being ridiculed, but it is the fact that they probably could not care less about how I feel and could do little to make me feel any different.

Wherever the Spirit of the Lord is, men's souls are set free.
—2 Corinthians 3:17 JBP

Psychology tells us we have four basic feelings and a whole host of periphery feelings. The primary feelings are *sad, mad, glad,* and *scared.* (No, *tired* is not one of them.) At different times of the day, these feelings pop up with little warning. Someone's painful story makes us feel sad. Someone cuts us off on the freeway and we get mad. We win a prize in a local contest and we feel glad. The IRS calls and we feel scared.

We ask groups a question in our workshops: "How do you feel about your former spouse?" (We usually ask this when things are dull.) It is definitely a feelings-raising question, which receives loud and differing responses. Mad comes up more often than glad.

Feelings are neither right nor wrong—they just are. We can choose to repress them or express them. We often feel better when we have talked about them to another person. While other people cannot make the feelings go away, they can acknowledge them and even empathize with us.

God, set me free to share my heart with others who will understand.

Having feelings is human. Expressing them is taking ownership of them. We are made in God's image, with the full range of feelings that He has given us.

God sets you free today to share your feelings. It can cleanse some of the emotional logjams of your life.

Home again

The story in the Honolulu newspaper captured my attention. It was about a home for runaway teenagers, a place where they could feel safe, get questions answered, and begin to rebuild their lives. The house had a huge sign hanging over the front door, which read, *Ka Hale Ake Ola.* The words mean, "The house that desires life." Can you envision that sign hanging over the front door of your home, condo, or apartment? It would certainly say something positive about the people who live there.

Divorce rearranges housing accommodations. You may go from a four bedroom, three bath house in a middle-class suburb to a one bedroom, one bath apartment by the freeway. The sense of home and security that you once had is usually lost, and you may feel like a displaced refugee.

Following divorce, you can choose to live a transient existence, or you can settle in and give life and meaning to your new residence. This is especially important if you have children. Home is an anchor for them. They need its security when they are experiencing so many changes in their lives.

There is a powerful promise in today's scripture. People are often prisoners in many ways prior to a divorce. Some are in physical prisons, while others are in emotional prisons. Many homes prior to divorce are filled with violence, anger, and chaos. Although leaving that kind of home can mean a loss, God promises to lead the prisoners to happy freedom.

Begin today to have a home that desires life, no matter what your address is.

God makes a home for the lonely; He leads out the prisoners into prosperity.
—Psalm 68:6
NASB

God, I know that someday I will be at home with You. Until then, help me to have the happiest home I can in this life.

Have you seen any angels lately?

What does an angel look like? Wispy wings, a gossamer robe, a halo, and a smile? Throw in a harp for good measure, and many would say you have a composite of an angel.

What does an angel do? Sit on your shoulder? Fly through the heavens? Keep bad things from befalling you?

If you believe all of the above, you have probably been watching too many movies and television shows.

I believe in angels, but I believe they defy description and easy identification. I believe God uses them in many ways, although they remain unseen to the naked eye. Which means they remain more of a mystery. Unless they come in human form.

Have you seen any angels in human form lately? Most of us have at some point in our lives, otherwise we wouldn't say to someone, "You are an angel!" We say those words to someone who has done something kind for us. No halo and no harp, just a bearer of human kindness and love.

I believe God sends angels in human form to us when we need them most. Some are there for us briefly, and then they are gone. Others stay around for a longer time and help us in our healing and growth. God sends you angels when you are going through the pain and loss of divorce. Even the psalmist was aware of them when he said, "He shall give His angels charge over you, to keep you in all your ways."

The old spiritual says, "All day, all night, angels watchin' over me my Lord." Keep your eyes open today for the appearance of God's angels in your life.

He shall give His angels charge over you, to keep you in all your ways.
—Psalm 91:11
NKJV

God, I could use a few guardian angels in my life right now. Surround me with the protective care I need as I face my pain and loss.

Living beyond blame

Little children learn to play the blame game when they are quite young. When accused of doing something wrong, they first say that they did not do it. When that won't solve things, they resort to blaming someone else. We have years to practice that procedure and hone our skills at deflecting blame.

How does blaming someone else help us? It doesn't. It makes us weaker, not stronger. Author Steven Covey says, "Many divorced people are still consumed with anger and bitterness and self-justification regarding a former spouse. In a negative sense, psychologically, they are still married . . . they each need the weakness of the former partner to justify their accusations."

Do you spend time blaming your former spouse or someone else for all your troubles? If you do, you are wasting a lot of energy and time at a game you cannot win. Blaming is a mental and emotional sport for many people. They play the script out in their heads and then verbalize it when they see their former spouse. The end result is a lengthy verbal battle with no resolution other than exhaustion.

We all play the blame game at one time or another. It is a form of self-vengeance that only deepens wounds. Today's scripture advises us to leave all revenge up to the Lord. Release your desire to play the blame game today, and let God be responsible for repayment. Learn to say, "That's God's problem!"

Dear friends, never avenge yourselves. Leave that to God, for he has said that he will repay those who deserve it.
—Romans 12:19 TLB

God, I confess I would like to get back at those who have hurt me. Help me to leave that up to You and focus on my own growth and needs.

It is embarrass-ing to be a beginner

I don't like to admit that I will always be a beginner at some things. After all, I am fifty-something. I began my earthly journey a long time ago. By now I should specialize in endings, not beginnings. Beginnings make you feel as though you don't know anything and must rely on others to learn. They make you feel insecure and tentative and often just plain dumb. I feel much better and wiser when I can convince others I am a veteran, not a beginner.

Divorce is for beginners. No matter how many years you were married, you start over again after a divorce. Many people who are newly divorced don't even want to talk about starting over. They are embarrassed by the dissolution of their marriage and would rather not be called to any new beginnings at this point in their lives.

Starting over is like being in a halfway house. You are not where you were, and you are not where you want to be. You want to move ahead without making any mistakes. Everyone appears to be watching you. You know that some are cheering for you, whereas others are ignoring you completely.

One workshop participant summed it up this way: "I've learned many things about myself living alone. I'm the same, yet I'm different. No one can be a substitute for that part of me that is gone. My void is being filled in a new way. I'm becoming more totally me—halfway between where I've been and where I'm going."

If today is your first step toward a new beginning, let God direct that step.

A man's heart plans his way, but the LORD directs his steps.
—Proverbs 16:9
NKJV

God, I will always be a beginner. Walk with me and guide my steps today.

What kind of deal are you looking for?

The angry woman expressed her feelings about her divorce very forcibly and succinctly. She said, "This is a terrible ordeal that has shattered my ideal, and now I am looking for a new deal!" She probably summed up about 90 percent of all the feelings of the more than one and a quarter million people who got divorced last year. Everyone I know who enters marriage has an ideal they hold before them. When the ideal fails, divorce is often not far behind. Some ideals are well beyond the realm of fulfillment, whereas others are so low there is nothing to work toward.

Many divorces become ordeals. Whether they are brief, or long and drawn out, the human energy they demand makes them trials both in and out of the courtroom. Divorce is often dehumanizing and debilitating. If it does not consume you emotionally, it will engulf you financially.

After several months of recovery, many formerly marrieds are looking for something a whole lot better than what they had: a new deal with a new person and a whole new life. Many secretly wonder what will happen if they remarry.

Often, the ideals in a second or third marriage also crumble and another divorce ensues. New relationships need to be built upon strong foundations. A person must learn everything he or she can about the failed marriage before saying "I do" again. The lessons of divorce are more often learned in recovery programs than in new marriages.

An ideal, an ordeal, or a new deal is no deal at all unless it is God's deal! Today's scripture promises God's guidance as we work toward building a new life and new relationships.

I will instruct you and teach you in the way you should go; I will guide you with My eye.
—Psalm 32:8 NKJV

God, teach me what I need to learn from my past relationship, and guide me and go before me as I move toward new ones.

It's a Charlie Brown world

Charlie Brown, the some-time hero and sometime scapegoat of the *Peanuts* comic strip, says, "I need all the friends I can get!" I follow his travails in life each day in the morning paper. I often wonder how he can put up with the subversive antics of some of the other characters that tromp through his life.

"Follow me . . . and I will make you fishers of men."
—*Mark 1:17*
NIV

The popular comic strip is a parody of life. At one time or another, we can all identify with Charlie Brown and his friends. Like Charlie Brown, you and I need our support systems to validate and contribute to our growth and development.

Divorce often shakes a person's friendship tree, and many former friends fall right out of your life. New friends enter and bring with them the emotional qualities you need while you are in recovery. One of the things I have learned about building support systems is to keep your heart and arms open for the people God is sending in your direction. Too many of us close down in fear of further rejection or abuse. I believe you need to be cautious, careful, and prayerful as you build new friendships.

God, some days I feel I have lost more than I have gained. Help me to be a part of the people who follow You as I rebuild my world.

Just as Charlie Brown's friends sometimes irritate him, members of our support systems can sometimes irritate us by directing our attention to a character flaw or destructive pattern we are repeating. But in a healthy support group, even criticism is given out of love and with our best interests at heart.

I liken Charlie Brown's crew to the first disciples. They were a group of misfits, but Jesus saw them for what they could become. When they followed Him, their lives were forever changed.

Your life can be changed today by following Jesus and opening yourself to the friends He sends your way.

Where do I go to surrender?

Do you remember the story of the Japanese soldiers who were found hiding years after World War II ended? No one had told them the war was over. They lived in fear of capture and death for many years, not knowing that they were free because their country had surrendered to the American forces.

The place of surrender can be a doorway to freedom and a new life. Divorce can be likened to surrender in many ways. Many men and women are prisoners of dysfunctional marriages. When a decision is made to save one's self and surrender the marriage, a new ray of hope can beam into your life.

We tell men and women in our seminars that a person must do everything he or she can to save the marriage before surrendering and moving on. The truth is, it takes work on the part of both husband and wife to heal a troubled relationship. One alone cannot do it (even though many people think they can.) When a person has done all he or she can to get help and the other partner refuses, the marriage will end.

Surrendering when you had hoped to win takes a great amount of courage. We all secretly pray for miracles and change in another person. When they don't come, surrender can feel more like defeat than a window of opportunity to a new life.

Surrendering is not always giving up on someone or something. It can mean choosing a new pathway for yourself and making the other person responsible for his or her own problems. When you surrender you might need a hiding place for a time. Today's verse is God's way of providing that.

You are my hiding place; You shall preserve me from trouble; You shall surround me with songs of deliverance.
—Psalm 32:7 NKJV

God, I claim You today as my hiding place. Thank You for surrounding me with Your love and care.

When you feel branded

He looked me in the eye and said, "I feel branded. Everywhere I go I feel like I have a big *D* in the middle of my forehead. Should I run away, grow long hair down my forehead, or just practice my lying?"

There are a lot of divorced people out there who can identify with this man's comment. You probably can also. There are some days when you feel that no matter where you go or who you are with, everyone around you knows you are divorced. You feel as though little ultrasonic waves are emanating from your person and silently announcing to the whole world that you are a branded person.

Being married lets the world know that you have someone special in your life, and you don't have to search for a relationship. Divorce says you lost what you had, so you must now be a loser and wear the brand.

Divorce is a disappointment that brings with it a lot of disgrace. You can be beaten down by it, or you can ask the Lord to help you go through it. Today's verse tells us that with the Lord's help, we will not be disgraced or ashamed. That's a powerful promise for those who brand themselves and allow others to brand them as failures.

Hold your head high today because the Lord will help you.

"For the Lord GOD will help Me; therefore I will not be disgraced; therefore I have set My face like a flint, and I know that I will not be ashamed."
—Isaiah 50:7
NKJV

God, I confess to You I feel ashamed as I go through this divorce. Help me to reject the brand of failure and trust You for healing.

42

The touch that heals

Children of all ages get lost in a divorce. While parents are squabbling and scrambling to work out a divorce settlement, children are pushed into the background and told not to worry about anything. Very few parents tell their children exactly what is happening and listen to their concerns.

And He took them up in His arms, laid His hands on them, and blessed them.
—Mark 10:16 NKJV

When a family system disintegrates, children have a right to know how their lives will be affected. They also need to know that they will be loved and cared for and that no one will divorce them—ever!

Over the years I have watched thousands of children try to process their parents' divorce. During single parent retreats I have watched the children of single mothers spend most of their time with the men because they have little or no relationship with a male figure in their lives. I have watched the children of single fathers do the same thing with the women at a retreat. All of these children were desperately saying, "Will you love and accept me and let me hug and hang on to you for a while?"

There is a powerful example of the needs of all children in today's scripture. Little children were brought to Jesus so that He might simply touch them, and in so doing, bless them. The disciples responded to the intrusion by rebuking the people who brought the children. Jesus told them, "Let the little children come to Me . . . for of such is the kingdom of God" (Mark 10:14 NKJV). Then He touched them and blessed them.

God, help me to be sensitive today to my children.

How long has it been since you responded to your children's needs as Jesus did? A touch, a hug, some real conversation with them is vital to their existence and yours. It really doesn't matter how little or how big they are—just do it!

Duck! They are shooting the wounded!

The following letter was sent to me through my publisher. I have read many letters like it before and experienced the same heaviness in my heart.

My husband has left me for someone else, and I am going through a divorce. We have both been in our church for many years and active in many different programs. When the pastor heard about our divorce, he asked me to no longer continue in any leadership programs so that our church would not be embarrassed by my impending divorce. He even subtly suggested I might be happier in another church.

If you were or still are a part of a church that cares for and helps heal its wounded, you might wonder if churches like the one described in the letter really exist. Sadly, they do, and the pain they inflict on their people who are wounded by divorce is cruel and inhuman. I have told my share of wounded to pack up and find a new church immediately if this ever happens to them.

Henri Nouwen says, "A Christian community is therefore a healing community, not because wounds are cured and pains are alleviated, but because wounds and pains become openings for a new vision." Nouwen adds further that we are all "wounded healers."

Some churches and some church people still choose to shoot their wounded in the name of biblical fundamentals. They somehow feel that if God hates divorce (which He does), they should in turn hate all divorced people (which God doesn't).

Run when those people shoot at you, and claim God's promise today from the Psalms. God protects you not only from the enemy, but also from some people armed with good intentions.

He protects you day and night. He keeps you from all evil, and preserves your life. He keeps his eye upon you as you come and go, and always guards you.
—Psalm 121:6–8 TLB

God, help me to forgive those who have made my injuries worse and draw around me those who can aid in my healing.

Looking for a quiet center

Have you ever been to a place of great beauty and stillness and had the overwhelming desire to plant yourself right in the middle of it? I felt that way two years ago when I toured the fjords of Norway. It was so majestic and quiet that I wanted to stay forever. I just knew I would become a quieter and perhaps gentler person living deep inside the peaks and valleys of Scandinavia.

There is little peace during a divorce. Your inner world can be as turbulent as your outer world. Family life can be a whirlwind all by itself. The treadmill keeps running, and the noise it produces is deafening. If you find a quiet center, chances are you are soon disturbed, as though you were sitting in the eye of a hurricane and the winds resumed.

But don't give up. Today's verse tells us that we will come to know God in stillness. That is when we can really hear God speak to us. We have to turn off all the sounds around us and make a quiet center in our hearts and minds for God to enter. In silence and solitude God can transform our lives.

Will you give God some quiet corners in your busy life?

Be still, and know that I am God.
—Psalm 46:10
NKJV

God, calm my turbulent spirit today with Your holy presence.

45

When your parents don't understand

I will never forget the parents who came to my office one day to talk about their son's divorce. Their question was, "What did we do wrong in our child's life that could have caused this divorce to happen?" I wish I could have thought of a clever answer to assuage their guilt. Their son had been married and away from his parents' home for years and years. In fact, the son lived in another state. Yet they still felt somehow guilty for his divorce.

A parent is a parent forever. You go through whatever your children go through regardless of their ages. Your inherent desire is that they might be happy in life, have no tragedies, and bless you with many healthy grandchildren.

Parents will always feel guilty where their children are concerned. It is the parent disease that has no known cure. Death is the only thing that terminates guilt.

Children need to talk with their parents when they experience divorce and parents need to lovingly talk with their children. The love that each has for the other can be an anchor in a divorce storm. Too many parents and children abandon each other due to divorce misunderstandings. Building bridges here will take some time and patience, but it is worth the effort.

If you feel deserted by your parents or family, claim the verse from scripture today as your own. God will sustain you.

For if my father and mother should abandon me, you would welcome and comfort me.
—Psalm 27:10 TLB

God, help me today to have better relationships with my children and my parents.

Scheduling personal time

When was the last time you had some time to yourself? Last month? Last year? Has it been so long you don't remember? Many companies allow their employees to take "personal time" off from work. When you take it, you don't have to come to work, and you don't have to call in and say you are sick when you are not. Personal time means you have some things to take care of, and you don't have to tell anyone what they are.

Personal time is *not* for frantically trying to catch up with all your undone chores. It is reserving some time to reflect, meditate, read, think, or work on a personal growth project. These things are vital to your serenity.

Jesus spent long days talking to people and healing them of many different infirmities. He knew He needed stillness and prayer to renew Himself. He could not keep going without it. And neither can you. Take a look at your calendar today and schedule some time apart for yourself.

And He said to them, "Come aside by yourselves to a deserted place and rest a while."
—Mark 6:31
NKJV

God, help me realize the importance of time apart from all my pressures. Help me today to plan for it when I need it.

Take God with you

There is probably no experience more intimidating than a job interview. I was in an office building in our town recently and noticed a whole row of people filling out job applications in a corner of the lobby. I watched them as I waited for the elevator. Some hurried to fill out the forms while others took their time and kept looking around the lobby to see if anyone was watching them. One woman reduced her nail length bite by bite. All of them looked uncomfortable.

"Have I not commanded you? Be strong and of good courage; do not be afraid, nor be dismayed, for the LORD your God is with you wherever you go."
—Joshua 1:9
NKJV

Many newly divorced men and women must search for new employment. Often, a divorced person needs a higher paying job to compensate for the loss of the ex-spouse's income. Many older women who are divorced after a long-term marriage must enter or reenter the workforce, and they quickly discover that today's job market is very competitive.

Feelings of fear and self-doubt can overwhelm you when you seek new employment. You fear being rejected by a prospective employer. If you do get rejected, your self-confidence can suffer, and you feel even more fear and self-doubt at your next interview.

When you go job hunting, you can't take your friends and relatives with you. No one is there to hold your hand and calm your spirit. No personal cheerleaders surround you with affirming words. You may feel all alone. But today's verse assures you that there is Someone who promises to go with you and give you the strength and confidence you need. Many years ago, Joshua had just gotten a new job. He took over when Moses died. Joshua experienced tremendous self-doubt. God promised Joshua that he would go nowhere and do nothing alone. God would go with him. That same promise is yours today. Do you believe it?

God, job interviews are stressful. When I go on my next one, I invite You to go with me.

48

Dump your garbage

Years of unresolved conflict in a person's life can result in one colossal pile of garbage. After a while, the stench of that garbage can follow you everywhere you go. It will smell up not only your life, but the lives of everyone with whom you come in contact.

I am discovering that many divorcing people are working through not only their divorce, but also years of accumulated emotional garbage. Sexual abuse, physical abuse, and emotional abandonment are only a few of the more common things. Adult children of alcoholics often find a lot of emotional lint clinging to them after a divorce. If such dysfunctions are not resolved, they can be passed on to future generations.

Counseling, therapy, self-study, and hard work all help when it comes to dumping garbage. It takes strong personal commitment and the willingness to invest whatever time it takes. Problems accumulated over many years cannot be resolved in a few days.

When you dump the garbage from your life, you make room for good things. I frequently see people genuinely excited by their new growth. They soon come to a point when they say, "How did I live so long with all that garbage?"

Our lives are changed forever whenever healing takes place. It is then that God can fill us with the fruits of the spirit described in today's scripture. Are you willing to trade in some old garbage that is gumming up your life for the gifts God is offering to you? Recovery is a long process, but you can get started now!

But the fruit of the Spirit is love, joy, peace, longsuffering, kindness, goodness, faithfulness, gentleness, self-control. Against such there is no law.
—Galatians 5:22–23
NKJV

God, help me to stop collecting garbage. Guide me into new life and growth.

When you need protection

Fear not, for I am with you; be not dismayed, for I am your God. I will strengthen you, yes, I will help you, I will uphold you with My righteous right hand.
—Isaiah 41:10 NKJV

Dealing with a vindictive spouse can be frightening. Often an order of protection must be obtained from the local police or sheriff's office to guarantee that an act of violence will not take place between two estranged spouses. Tragically, these orders are often not observed, and physical violence or even death is the outcome.

My advice in seminars over the years in this area has been simple. Never take threats lightly, and protect yourself whenever you feel your life is in danger. We never know how another person will respond when emotions and feelings are pushed to the limit.

We all need to be reassured of God's protection in our lives. We pray daily that God will protect us and our family and friends from any and all forms of bodily harm. As the level of fear rises in our society, we become more conscious of our need to walk closer to God each day.

The words of the prophet Isaiah can give us the courage to leave our place of refuge each day and walk into our world without fear. In the highways and hallways of our lives, God promises to go with us and strengthen us. When we cannot hold ourselves up, He promises to uphold us. When we need protection from anyone or anything, He promises to help us. God's promise of protection is lasting and permanent.

God, go with me each day into my world and protect me from those who would hurt me. May my growing trust in You put all my fears to rest.

When you want to be real

I end my divorce recovery workshops with a reading from one of my favorite children's books, *The Velveteen Rabbit* by Margery Williams. It sums up what all the participants struggle with—how to be real in the unreal world of divorce.

"Do not be unbelieving, but believing."
—John 20:27
NKJV

"What is REAL?" asked the Rabbit one day, when they were lying side by side near the nursery fender, before Nana came to tidy the room. "Does it mean having things that buzz inside you and a stick-out handle?"

"Real isn't how you are made, " said the Skin Horse. "It's a thing that happens to you. When a child loves you for a long, long time, not just to play with, but REALLY loves you, then you become real."

"Does it hurt?" asked the Rabbit.

"Sometimes," said the Skin Horse, for he was always truthful. "When you are Real you don't mind being hurt."

"Does it happen all at once, like being wound up," he asked, "or bit by bit?"

"It doesn't happen all at once," said the Skin Horse. "You become. It takes a long time. That's why it doesn't happen to people who break easily, or have sharp edges, or have to be carefully kept. Generally, by the time you are Real, most of your hair has been loved off, and your eyes drop out and you get loose in the joints and very shabby. But these things don't matter at all, because once you are Real you can't be ugly, except to people who don't understand."

God, being real is often painful. Help me to know that I am real and loved by You.

Hooked on a feeling

I like the oldies radio station in my town. Those tunes take me back to simpler times when the world wasn't shaking and breaking. I heard one of my favorite songs recently. I can't remember all the words, but the chorus says, "I'm hooked on a feeling . . . I'm still in love with you."

But the greatest of these is love.
—1 Corinthians 13:13 NKJV

What happens when you still love your former spouse, but he or she doesn't still love you? The reality is that divorce doesn't always mean the end of love. I have talked with people who have been divorced for ten or more years who admit to still loving their ex-spouse. Is that love lost or wasted? I don't think so.

When you love someone, that is not always changed by something he or she does to you or you do to him or her. That love is usually stored away in a special place in your heart. Good memories have made it a special treasure that you will always possess. It won't be on the front burner of your life everyday, and it won't become a possessive or compulsive thing. And it won't necessarily disappear when you marry another person. It can remain forever in the archives of your heart.

God, it's hard to let go of love. Please help me where it hurts!

Many divorced people feel guilty when they confess to still being in love with a former spouse, especially one who has brought great pain to their lives. The truth is, you feel what you feel, and most of the time those feelings are not right or wrong—they just are. Don't feel bad about any leftover love you might still have. Real love is pretty tenacious!

Affordable therapy

Have you ever struggled with admitting you were wrong in a certain situation? Remember how hard it was? Wouldn't it be great to always be right and never have to confess that you were wrong?

As humans, we all have to deal with the conflict between right and wrong. God seemed to know that we would make mistakes, so He provided a way to help us take care of them. His formula is simple: confession equals cleansing and forgiveness. It's not an easy formula to live with, but it is the only one that helps us keep a right relationship with both God and other people.

Today's scripture is a powerful challenge. It says, "If we confess our sins, He is faithful and just to forgive us our sins and to cleanse us from all unrighteousness." You will notice this verse begins with the word *if.* That might prompt you to ask what happens if we don't confess our sins. From my experience, lack of confession leads to guilt, anger, and depression.

Many of us cart around sins that we need to confess to God. Only when we confess them and own up to them can God do anything with them. His promise becomes a cleansing therapy that will make us whole again if only we will practice confession and forgiveness in our lives.

As we confess our wrongs to God and ask His forgiveness, we have to take it to the next level and ask forgiveness from people we have hurt.

Confession is the heart's cry for cleansing and wholeness. Forgiveness is the act of restoring broken relationships. It can be a painful process, but the seeds of confession and forgiveness grow well in the gardens of our lives.

Is it time for you to confess your wrongs to God and other people? Is it time for you to forgive the people who have hurt you?

If we confess our sins, He is faithful and just to forgive us our sins and to cleanse us from all unrighteousness.
—1 John 1:9
NKJV

God, make me sensitive today to the wrongs I need to deal with. Give me the strength to obey You.

Making your own decisions

Are you the kind of person who has difficulty making decisions? Do you put them off as long as you can or try to get others to make your decisions for you?

Decision making becomes more difficult after a divorce. A mate who once helped you make decisions or made them all for you is no longer around. There is no one to consult with or take responsibility for decisions. Tragically, in many marriages decision making has been a one-sided affair for many years.

For many single-again men and women, this becomes a major issue in the struggle to survive divorce. For a while, the fear of making the wrong decisions outweighs the joy of making the right decisions. Slowly one learns the joy and risk of making a decision without help from a spouse. You may even discover that you are totally capable of making good decisions.

We all need outside help and wisdom in the important decisions of life. Good friends can provide valuable input and guidance. But it is not their responsibility to make our decisions for us. After we do the homework, we alone have to finish the assignment.

I believe good decision making comes through the share and prayer process. It does not come from one person telling another person what to do and when to do it.

Today's scripture tells us to ask God for whatever things we need and believe that He will answer our prayers. Ask God today to guide you in your decision making, and then believe that you can and will make the right decisions.

"Therefore I say to you, whatever things you ask when you pray, believe that you receive them, and you will have them."
—Mark 11:24
NKJV

God, it's hard for me to make my own decisions. Help me to believe that with Your guidance I can make the right decisions today.

Remember, you are a person

The statement was born early in the age of computerization and automation. You may remember it: "I am a person! Do not fold, bend, staple, stamp, or mutilate me in any way."

The expression of personhood is vital to human survival. The containment or oppression of personhood causes death to the soul and spirit. Divorce often sets people free who have lived in oppressive marriages. Slowly they discover that someone took away their personhood and now they are getting it back.

The freedom of reclaiming my personhood means many things, including:

not letting others put me in a box.
not always being predictable.
letting the inside of me come outside.
expressing my talents and gifts.
learning to stretch beyond my known capacity.
letting others be who they are.
thanking God for the gift of being me.

That's a good checklist for you to look at today. How are you doing in reclaiming your personhood? God's wish for you is that you might know who you are, express yourself fully, and live life more abundantly. That is the promise in today's scripture. God's gift to you today is *life!*

"I have come that they may have life, and that they may have it more abundantly."
—*John 10:10*
NKJV

God, thank You for creating me in Your image. Help me to reclaim Your creativity today.

Who is that in your mirror?

When we were children we played make-believe games. We dressed up in our parents' old clothes and pretended we were adults. We went to movies and came away playing the part of the screen hero. We pretended we were Superman, Cinderella, or some other character from a cartoon or storybook. We pretended to be like our heroes, whether they were real or fictional. They were our role models.

There is nothing wrong with having a role model. Most of us are composites of many different people we have admired in our lives. There is something wrong, however, when we try to be something or someone we are not. Many divorced women have said that they tried to be the perfect housewife and mother. Likewise, many divorced men have often said that they tried to be the perfect father.

Divorce can challenge your self-image, whether real or imagined. You may ask yourself, "Who am I?" You may struggle to authenticate your identity.

One woman recently told me that being divorced is like looking in the mirror and seeing yourself for the first time. I asked her what she said when she saw herself. Her response was simply, "Wow!" I suggested that she also say these words the next time she looked in the mirror: "I am God's unique, unrepeatable miracle, and God loves me. He created *me* in His image."

Who do you see in your mirror?

So God created man in His own image; in the image of God He created him; male and female He created them.
—Genesis 1:27 NKJV

God, the next time I look in a mirror, help me to see myself as Your unique creation.

56

Good-bye security, hello challenge

We live in a security-oriented society. We secure our homes with burglar alarms. We try to find jobs that are secure from layoffs and mergers. We want better law enforcement so that we will be secure from crime. Somehow, we all feel more secure with more security.

God is our refuge and strength, a very present help in trouble. Therefore we will not fear, even though the earth be removed, and though the mountains be carried into the midst of the sea.
—Psalm 46:1–2 NKJV

Being divorced can make you feel very insecure. You may immediately search to find another husband or wife to restore the security you lost in your previous marriage. As a man at one of our workshops said, "I have to find someone to take care of me." You will note he did not say that he had to find someone to care for.

Growth after a divorce is not about looking for someone to give you a sense of security. It is learning to find security within yourself. This does not mean you will never need other people. It means that you reach down deeply into yourself and tap into the strength of your own resources.

Security is also putting your trust in God for His direction in your life. It is allowing Him to call forth what is often buried deep within you. In today's verse, God promises to be our refuge and strength. Knowing that, what have you to fear?

Good-bye security. Good-bye fear. Hello challenge. Hello God!

God, the next time I want to run and hide, help me to take Your hand and keep moving!

Don't put me in second class!

"I feel like a second-class Christian." I wish I had a quarter for each time I have heard that comment. One man said, "Bank robbers and murderers are more respected in our church than divorced folks!" It is a sad commentary on the state of church folk and Christians in general. It is easy to miss what the church and family of God is all about: loving and caring for those in pain.

Most divorcing people know that divorce is wrong in God's eyes. It certainly was not part of God's perfect plan for married men and women. Many of the people I meet had little or no say in their divorce. Their marriage ended because their spouse made the decision. Should they now be relegated to a second-class existence in their church and Christian community? I personally don't believe so. Divorce is not the unforgivable sin. It is a human sin, and forgiveness is readily available.

There are scores of committed Christians sitting on the sidelines today because someone decided that divorce made them second-class citizens. Even though more and more churches are caring and helping to heal the pain of divorce in their ranks, the labeling of divorced persons as second-class Christians will be around for a long time to come. I caution you not to fall victim to it. God doesn't put anyone in a class. He accepts all of us just as we are—that includes you!

"I demand that you love each other as much as I love you."
—*John 15:12*
TLB

God, I thank You today that I will always be in first class in Your eyes, because Your love paid the fare.

Little hooks and big memories

The caller said, "I think I'm cracking up! I just fell apart at a stoplight and had to pull off the road. I sat in my car and cried for twenty minutes before I could go on. Am I okay?"

The woman went on to tell me that when she stopped at the light, she saw a favorite restaurant where she and her ex-husband had spent many happy celebrations and hours. As her memory went backward, her tears came forward.

I told her that she was not cracking up but had merely had a little memory hook from yesterday reach out and snag her. I also told her it was okay to respond the way she did, and that memories are real and don't disappear when one goes through a divorce.

What do you do with the happy memories of a marriage that ended in divorce? What do you do with the sad memories? You file them in your mind and spirit and realize they are the collectibles of life. They don't dissolve and go away. They are with you always.

Recalling good memories can make us feel sad. We want to return to those good times. Perhaps it is easier to deal with bad memories. We can just get mad and be glad those times are over.

God has gifted us with memories. It is the way we can measure our progress in life and evaluate our dreams. Living each day is the making of a memory. Good and bad are side by side. Growth is making peace with the bad memories and recalling the good ones with a spirit of celebration.

Struggling with memories may make us feel weak, but God comes closer to each of us when we struggle and gives us His strength.

For when I am weak, then I am strong.
—2 Corinthians 12:10 NKJV

God, thank You for memories that reflect my journey.

Where to from here?

If divorce is a time of chaos and craziness, it is also a time of exploring new options and directions for your life. It is time to review your life and ask the question, "Where to from here?" For the Christian, it is time to go to God and ask Him to help you know His plans for your life.

God wants us to be adventurers in finding out what He wants us to do in every area of our lives. It might be changing jobs, changing friends, or just making a change in everyday actions.

Finding out what God wants you to do should not be a complex task. You need not read twenty books on how to know God's will. God doesn't specialize in confusing us and placing obstacles in our paths.

In today's verse, there is a simple guideline for knowing what God wants you to do in any area of your life: Trust the Lord and acknowledge Him, and He will direct you. If you stay on God's track, you will always receive the guidance you need in every area of your life.

Knowing what God wants us to do and doing it are two different things. I know many people who know God's orders but are reluctant to follow them. God gives the plan and the power to follow the plan a day at a time. Are you willing to accept God's plan for you today?

Trust in the LORD with all your heart, and lean not on your own understanding; in all your ways acknowledge Him, and He shall direct your paths.
—Proverbs 3:5–6 NKJV

God, help me to follow You one day at a time, starting right now.

Giving yourself away

The little sign had a big message: *Love Isn't Love till You Give It Away.* No one benefits from love that is stored up. It can only be appreciated when it is dispensed by one person and received by another. Love is not passive. Love is active. Gifts of love come in all shapes and sizes, and the best kinds are usually covered with skin.

Love is giving yourself away. When you are happy and times are good, that is easy to do. When life is tough and you are wading through crisis after crisis, you don't think much about dispensing love. You want to be a receiver.

Love is giving and receiving. Both can be difficult when you are hurting and someone has shattered a loving relationship that once was the center of your life. It is easy to build tall walls to protect yourself from further hurt. The danger of hiding behind those walls for too long is that you can develop a battered and bitter spirit and forever cut off the love lines in your life.

A vital part of healing your hurts is to risk reaching out to others. In a recent seminar, a woman approached me with tears in her eyes and commented on how much help she had received over the past six weeks from her small support group. My thoughts went back to the first night this group was together and the apparent distrust they had for one another. Now, six weeks later, they had cried and laughed together through many of their problems.

Today's scripture tells us that receiving comes from giving, even when you feel like you have nothing to give. All we need to do is take the initiative and trust God to start the river of giving flowing from us to others.

"Give, and it will be given to you." —Luke 6:38 NKJV

God, help me to give even when I feel I have nothing to give.

Living with loose ends

Are you a person who likes to keep all his options open? Or do you like to nail down decisions and get on with other things? Most of us fall into one group or the other. A healthy balance would be a little of both.

"Lord, I believe; help my unbelief!"
—*Mark 9:24*
NKJV

You may have discovered that there are still some loose ends to tie up, even after you sign your final divorce papers. I remember my sister calling me when her divorce was finally over and telling me she would never have to see or deal with her former spouse again. But when her son got married, her ex-husband reappeared. Then he floated away, only to reappear when the grandchildren were born. She has finally come to the conclusion that her ex-husband will always be somewhere around the edges of her life because of her son.

You may ask, "When is my divorce final?" The truthful answer would probably be, "When you die." Divorce changes almost everything in your life, but it doesn't remove some things. There will be days when you will smile at all the continuing craziness and utter the simple prayer:

Lord, I believe that someday most of my divorce struggles will be behind me. Help me to trust You with the loose ends that remain.

Tough questions

There are some days when I wish I wouldn't have asked my seminar audience if they had any questions. The reason is that I am often asked tough questions that have either no answer or a painful answer. I would rather smile and tell everyone to "have a nice day."

Do all to the glory of God.
—1 Corinthians 10:31 NKJV

One of the toughest questions I hear is how does one deal with sexuality after divorce. What these people are really asking is if it's okay to have sexual relationships outside marriage.

This is an old question. Society at large battles with the ethics and morals of human sexuality. Like many other things, it's not a problem until *you* have to deal with it and find an answer.

There are basically three attitudes regarding sex outside of marriage. The first is, if it feels good and two people agree, then it's okay to do it. The second is, it's okay if there is a meaningful relationship between the two people. The third attitude is that sex is a gift from God and should be experienced only within marriage.

The apostle Paul provides us with some guidelines for sexuality in his first letter to the Christians at Corinth (1 Cor. 6:13–20; 10:31). He reminds us that our bodies are temples of the Holy Spirit and that we should always glorify God in all we do.

God, help me to know Your answers to this tough question in my life.

If you are struggling with this issue today, I suggest that you talk to God about it and do some homework. God cares about your questions and desires the best for you in life.

Walking on the water

She was both angry and sad. Her husband had left her for another woman just three months before his retirement. All their plans to move to a resort area and spend the rest of their lives enjoying a hard-earned retirement had been finalized. But now he was gone, the retirement dream had vanished, and she was looking for a job at age sixty-two. Her final words to me were, "It's not fair!"

She was right. Her experience is repeated day by day as many long-term marriages end. Long-planned goals and dreams disappear in an instant and are replaced with a file of divorce papers. A well constructed game plan for togetherness and enjoyment is dashed against the rocks of reality.

It is hard and slow going to pull yourself together, change your plans, and rebuild your life by yourself. The real question for most men and women whose long-term marriages have ended may be, "Is there time for me to rebuild my life and dream new dreams?"

God is the author of new beginnings, and when He is in your life your potential is unlimited. You can only be limited by fear and lack of trust. God is never limited by *your* situations. If you trust in Him and walk with Him, you can walk on the water and never sink.

Will you take some time today to dream new dreams?

God . . . is able to do far more than we would ever dare to ask.
—*Ephesians 3:20 TLB*

God, as my old dreams die, help me to trust You for new ones.

From pits to pinnacles

It's called Pinnacle Peak, and it's a few miles northeast of Scottsdale, Arizona. When you first spot it in the distance, it looks like an ice-cream cone turned upside down with ice cream still running down the side. Recently I performed a wedding at a country club at the base of Pinnacle Peak. I wondered how hard it would be to climb the spindly peak, and what I could do when I got to the top. For a few moments, I could look down on the world and give a loud yell. Then I would have to descend back to ground level.

He lifted me out of the pit of despair.
—Psalm 40:2 TLB

Life is comprised of climbing mountains and climbing out of the pits. It is easier to start on ground level than below ground level. I meet many people going through divorce who never seem to get above ground and permanently dwell in the pits. They often feel they don't deserve anything better and are unwilling to do what it takes to get out of the pits. In fact, they try to drag people in with them so that they will have some company.

Are you living in the pits right now when you would rather be climbing toward the pinnacle?

There is some good news found in today's scripture for people in the pits. It says, "I waited patiently for God to help me; then he listened and heard my cry. He lifted me out of the pit of despair, out from the bog and the mire, and set my feet on a hard, firm path and steadied me as I walked along" (Psalm 40:1–2 TLB).

God, help me today to start giving up my pits for Your pinnacles.

Can you see God doing that for you? Close your eyes for a minute and visualize God's great hand picking you up out of your pit and placing you on solid ground. Remember, you can't climb the pinnacles until you get out of the pits.

Murphy's law, God's answer

Remember Murphy? He moved into your life one day when you weren't looking and made himself right at home. He likes living in your residence so much that you know he plans to stay for your entire lifetime. One version of Murphy's Law is, "If anything can go wrong, it will." Another version says, "If anything bad happens, look out. More will follow immediately."

He who is in you is greater than he who is in the world.
—1 John 4:4
NKJV

You may have felt recently that Murphy's Law and divorce formed a partnership. You may be wondering if you will ever get the Murphy Corporation into bankruptcy and out of your life. It is easy to spend your time fanning Murphy's flames. Bad things happen to all of us, but the person who has a bad experience and builds a succession of them in his mind before they happen is setting himself up for Murphy's invasion. Many people do that in divorce. They think their children will become delinquents because of their divorce; that no one will ever love them again, and they will lose their job and end up living on the street pushing a shopping cart.

The good news today is that God has an answer to Murphy's Law. God is more powerful than Murphy, and you no longer have to live in fear of bad things happening to you.

Remember today who is greater. When bad things happen, say out loud:

God, You are greater than all the bad things in my life. Help me not to worry about bad things happening to me.

Next time, I know what I want

We were doing our remarriage seminar in San Diego. After lunch, a group of people started talking and joking about the kind of person they would like to marry *if* they ever were to marry again. One person said she would like to marry a very sick millionaire, and everyone laughed. A man said he wanted to marry someone who was a better cook and home decorator than he was. After a few minutes, a soft voice said, "If I marry again, I want to marry a man who loves God above all else and lives for Him." No one said a word, but all the heads started nodding in the affirmative.

What kind of person would you like to marry if you marry again? I know, you are still working through the barbed wire of divorce right now, but dream a moment with me. It might be good to write something in your daily journal and see how that will change over the next year or two.

More second marriages fail today than first marriages. Something is going wrong somewhere. It may be that personal qualifications lessen the longer one looks and waits.

Standards are formed as personal growth takes place in your own life. The more you grow, the higher your standards. A person only gets in trouble when the standards are lowered.

Let me give you a benchmark to shoot for when you think way down the road. Today's scripture says, "In everything you do, put God first." That means *you.* Don't wait until you are hopelessly lost in a relationship to put God first. Start doing it now.

In everyth ... ... do, put God first, and he will direct you and crown your efforts with success.
—*Proverbs 3:6*
TLB

God, I want to put You first in everything in my life. If I marry again, I want it to be with a person who puts You first in life.

Sharing love in your home

Divorce is the harsh termination of a love relationship between two people. Love dies before a divorce takes place for some, love dies after a divorce for others, and for still others, love for a former spouse never dies. Battling the feeling of love in the divorce experience is usually on a par with Don Quixote fighting windmills in Cervantes's great work of literature.

"Love one another as I have loved you."
—John 15:12
NKJV

No matter where your love goes after a divorce, self-love and love for your children and family must continue. That's often difficult when you feel that your own well of love has run dry, and you see no way for it to be restored within the next few years.

Love, as expressed to those you care about in family and community, comes in three varieties. The first is called "If" love. It always has conditions attached to it. "I will love you if you get good grades, keep your room clean, don't get in trouble, do the right thing, treat me well, and so on."

A second kind of love is called "Because" love. It is a lot like the first kind of love, but "Because" love puts conditions up front, and the love is dispensed only after good things happen.

God, help me to practice unconditional love today to my children, family, and friends.

The third kind of love is called "Anyhow" love. It is unconditional and comes close to the agape love the Bible talks about. It is a tough kind of love because it says, "I will love you even if you fail in school, get caught shoplifting, or stay out all night." It is a love that is not based on acts or performances. It is there and always will be, no matter what happens.

What kind of love do you practice?

The unmailed letter

A number of years ago, I sent a man a letter that should have gone in my desk drawer and not in the U.S. mail. I wrote it in an angry moment. Weeks, then months went by, and I heard nothing from the person I sent the letter to. One year later, the recipient sent the letter back to me with no comment or response. As I re-read it, I could not believe that I had written it and mailed it. It was awful, and I felt terrible and immediately apologized. And I learned a big lesson. You can always write a letter in anger, but don't mail it. File it away.

We all need to vent our feelings, and writing them down is one way to express them. Over the years I have suggested that it is therapeutic to write a letter to your former spouse, expressing your feelings. In that letter, you can include your positive memories of the person, along with your negative memories. You can tell your ex-spouse how all those memories make you feel. You should include a spirit of forgiveness in your letter and express how you want to deal with your ex-spouse in the future. The key to writing a letter such as this is to make sure you get all your feelings down on paper. If you keep them buried inside you, writing will not help.

Today's scripture encourages us to not harbor angry emotions and feelings because they only upset us. Owning and expressing feelings gives us a new freedom and a clean emotional slate. When feelings are vented on paper, worry about them is removed.

Cease from anger, and forsake wrath; do not fret—it only causes harm.
—Psalm 37:8 NKJV

God, some days I feel lost in all my dammed-up feelings and emotions. Help me to express them in healthy ways and become a more whole person.

Learning to be tough and tender

She cried in my office. He cried in my seminar. They each told me they were beaten and battered from their divorces and had no one to share their struggles with. I asked them if they had children, and both said yes. I then asked if they had talked with their children and shared their feelings with them. Both said no and told me they had to be strong and not show their true feelings to their children. Wrong!

Many parents feel that they have to be superparents and never share their fears and weaknesses with their children. You present a false front to your children and give them the false idea that adults can handle anything and are oblivious to their feelings. As the old country and western song says, you're "laughing on the outside, crying on the inside."

Your children can be a tremendous source of strength to you if you will allow them to know how you feel. Honesty allows you the freedom to establish a game plan *together*. Remember, children are a part of the divorce experience, too. There are times when they need to be spectators, but there are more times when they need to be participants.

A sense of family is more important in a time of crisis than in a time of celebration. Today's scripture affirms the wisdom of God in placing us in families. We draw strength from each other, even if some of the others are our children.

God sets the solitary in families.
—Psalm 68:6 NKJV

God, thank You for my family. Help me to share honestly with them each day.

When one is a majority

The seminar had ended, and I told my audience to have a good week and be good to themselves. The following week when we regrouped, I asked different people to share something good and something bad from the past week. One woman jumped up and told me she had just returned from six days in Hawaii where she had gone all by herself, and she thanked me for pushing her into it. I did not recall telling anyone to go to Hawaii, and I told her that. She said, "You told me to be good to myself, and I wondered what I could do to respond. So I jumped on a plane the next morning and flew off for a week in Hawaii all alone. I returned just four hours ago, in time for this seminar. It was the first time I had ever done anything like that alone, and it was *wonderful*." Everyone in the audience applauded.

Many people have lived in unhappy marriages where they were told they could not do anything by themselves, or if they did do something, it would be a mess. As a result, they are convinced that they cannot do anything alone or right, and they withdraw into social and emotional isolation.

You may have bought into that myth and the slogan, "Somebody said it couldn't be done, so I didn't even try." It takes courage to break free and begin to do some things on your own.

The feeling of self-accomplishment is vital in improving your self-esteem. It replaces the I Can't tape with the Can Do message.

As you begin to do some things on your own, remember that God is with you always. You will never really be alone anywhere when you allow God to be with you.

"Lo, I am with you always."
—Matthew 28:20
NKJV

God, help me become a Can Do person today and know that You are with me.

71

Developing spiritual sensitivity

At a place called divorce, many divorcing people turn toward God for help. At the same time, some who have followed God in the past may turn away from Him. God may be the one they blame the divorce on because they prayed it would not happen and it did. A crisis like divorce can be a test of the depths of our spirituality.

There are two questions that help us grow closer to God in our times of trial and testing. Both demand that we become more sensitive to God. The first question is "What is God saying in my life right now?" We all have many thoughts and ideas swirling around in our conscious and unconscious mind. We suffer from scattered attention and blurred focus in our purpose and activities. It is difficult to turn everything off, focus on God and listen for His answer to our question. Listening will take time and effort on your part.

The second question is "What is God doing in my life right now?" Focusing on this question brings us to a daily awareness of God at work within us. Being sensitive in this area is also being willing to watch for the hand of God moving through all the facets of my life and Christian journey. If I am aware of what God is doing, I can cooperate with trust and confidence allowing Him to do even more.

Today's scripture affirms our walk with God as a process that unfolds a day at a time. As we know Him better, we will know better what He desires in our lives and how our needs will be met.

For as you know him better, he will give you, through his great power, everything you need for living a truly good life: he even shares his own glory and his own goodness with us!
—2 Pet. 1:3
TLB

God, help me to hear what You are saying so I will know what I am doing today.

When you need live prayer

I don't know how many times I have had people say to me, "I'll pray for you." I'm sure they mean it, but I wonder when and how often they will pray for me.

There are times in my life, and I am sure there are times in yours, when I would love to have someone pray for me *right now!* Not next week or when they get to church or the next time their small group meets, but at the present moment. I call it *right now, up close, and in your face praying.*

Many of us have grown up to be prayer shy. We have a hard time asking others to pray for us right now, and we have an even harder time praying for someone else.

There is a certain intimacy and power present when we pray for each other. Humanly we are saying that we are right there for the other person. Spiritually we are saying we believe God hears and answers our prayers, and we can pray with that belief enforcing our prayers.

Today's scripture affirms our need for confession, intercession, and healing. We all desire healing for our hurts. Because we are not called to be lone rangers, we need to be a part of each other's joys and sorrows, and we need to pray for one another.

Therefore, confess your sins to one another, and pray for one another, so that you may be healed. The effective prayer of a righteous man can accomplish much.
—James 5:16
NASB

God, help me today to ask for prayer when I need it and to pray for others when they need it.

The words that kill

"I'm leaving you! I don't want to be married to you anymore! I don't love you!"

Marie sobbed as she told me her husband shouted these words over his shoulder, slammed the front door, and drove away to what he proclaimed was his "new life." These parting words left Marie in a state of shock, asking the question that is never easily answered: Why me?

There is no emergency room for people wounded by divorce. There is no survival kit you can buy from the corner drugstore to see you through this tempestuous ordeal. There is no magician who can wave a wand and change your situation. So what is the first thing you can do when you know your marriage is ending and you're about to go through a divorce?

Stop long enough to put yourself in God's hands. Ask Him to grant you strength and courage to get through today and the uncertain days ahead. Let Him wrap the powerful promise of Proverbs 3:5–6 around your heart. What you will have to face will not disappear, but you can know that God will be by your side to guide you and go before you. Be aware that a scriptural promise is not an antidote to your struggle; it is the equipment to take you through the struggle and give you hope and a future beyond divorce.

Human words can kill a relationship and wound your spirit. God's promises can give new life and bring peace to a hurting heart.

Trust in the LORD with all your heart and lean not on your own understanding; in all your ways acknowledge him, and he will make your paths straight.
—Proverbs 3:5–6 NIV

God, I know that some questions will not be answered in this life. Help me to live knowing that some day You will fill in the blanks and answer my questions.

Don't panic— God's in charge

"It's tragic that at the moment of the biggest crisis of your life, you have to make the most important decisions you will every make regarding your future. Man, this is crazy time!" After the workshop participant said this, he threw his hands in the air and walked away to his car.

For God has not given us a spirit of fear, but of power and of love and of a sound mind.
—2 Timothy 1:7 NKJV

I understood his confusion and despair. Four children, a shared business, and two homes were up for grabs in his divorce. Lawyers on both sides were pressing for a settlement. Legal fees were piling up, and the mounting pressures had this man in a panic.

The pressure to make major decisions during the first year of a divorce may seem unbearable. Your emotions are in turmoil, and fear often becomes the controlling emotion each day. You fret over the right decisions and mentally exhaust yourself.

God's verse for today is one of the most powerful promises from Scripture. It tells us clearly that the spirit of fear and God's Spirit do not cohabit. God enables us to supplant fear with His gifts of power, love, and a sound mind. All three can enable anyone going through divorce to make the wise and right decisions if they will seek God's guidance and wisdom in making those decisions.

The spirit of power, love, and sanity do not come by divine injection. They come by our willingness to allow God to work in our lives on His timetable, not ours. Remember, God is never in a hurry. Give Him time to work in your life.

God, I confess I have too many decisions, too many struggles, and too little time. Help me to get on Your timetable and trust You for power, love, and sanity today.

Part of the family of God

The calls come into our office every week. The callers are both men and women. A frantic voice says, "My spouse just moved out and is filing for a divorce. What do I do now?"

There are many obvious answers, such as Don't panic, Hang in there, Pray, Don't move, I'll be right over, and Good riddance! The most important and sustaining answer is to reach out to your supportive friends and ask them to hang on to you. If you have a church family that you belong to, that is the best place to seek support, love, and understanding. Contact your pastor immediately, and make him (or her) aware of your situation. Give your pastor the opportunity to counsel with you and help you develop a strategy for the coming days and weeks. Ask Him to support you prayerfully and point you to a divorce support group.

If the Christian community is anything, it is a healing community where you can take your pains, struggles, and questions and begin to seek wholeness. As a member of God's family, you have a right to ask for love, support, and help from the other members. That will not be easy, because divorce tends to throw a blanket of shame over one's life, and people who don't understand your need may add to your shame.

Over the years I have listened to many people who have expressed thanks for their church family, who supported them when they were going through a divorce. If your church doesn't reach out to you, take the initiative and ask for help.

Once you were not a people, but now you are the people of God; once you had not received mercy, but now you have received mercy.
—1 Peter 2:10 NIV

God, it is hard to feel defeated as a Christian. It is even harder to ask my church family for help. Give me the courage to ask them for their love and affirmation in the midst of my confusion and pain.

Little things mean a lot

Finding a book on my bookshelves these days is a major chore. My bookshelves are cluttered with assorted memorabilia from seventeen years of traveling and thirty-six years of marriage. These collectibles have no monetary value, but they have great sentimental value.

Your house or apartment probably looks like my bookshelves, so don't laugh. If a fire threatened your house or mine, we would probably grab all the little sentimental things and run for the door.

When you're hurting, little things mean a lot. Small acts of kindness can outweigh tons of despair. A dear friend of mine wrote the following poem. It says what most of us feel about little things.

A simple touch, really not much,
A word, a smile, a listening ear.
We think of greatness, kings and such,
We miss the truth, the point, I fear.
The thing that helps the hurting heart,
that comforts and lifts the wounded soul
Is not the great and powerful start
but little things that make us whole.
The cool drink given to your parched need,
That brought relief, the hope of renewal.
It's now your turn to plant the seed,
Those simple ways . . . a precious jewel.
—*Dennis Miller*

And he said to him, "Well done, good servant; because you were faithful in a very little, have authority over ten cities."
—*Luke 19:17 NKJV*

God, You created everything big and small. Help me today to appreciate the little things I've received and never undervalue them.

Hanging tough

Tough Times Never Last, But Tough People Do! I saw this title in a bookstore recently. In many ways I had said it to thousands of seminar participants over the years. Most of us would agree with the pronouncement, and all of us would ask the question, How long will the tough times last?

By now you have learned that living through divorce is living through the toughest time of your life. That time can often last two or three years, or even longer. You soon begin to wonder if you are really tough enough to endure this divorce triathlon that has no visible finish line.

James has a word of promise and hope for anyone going through the toughest of times. He calls them testing times, when your faith is stretched to the limit. For most divorced people I know, the limit is reached each day when they fall into bed exhausted.

James tells us there is a payoff for living through tough times. You will be the recipient of an endurance award! Once you have received that award, you will grow in maturity and wisdom. To state it simply: You won't grow much in life if you aren't battered, beaten, and bruised by the process.

We will never know how strong we are until that strength is tested. That strength will only increase *when* it is tested.

Many divorced people just want to survive their divorce and move on with their life. Only a few want to allow the experience to make them stronger, wiser, and more mature.

Consider it all joy, . . . when you encounter various trials, knowing that the testing of your faith produces endurance. And let endurance have its perfect result, that you may be perfect and complete, lacking in nothing.
—James 1:2–4
NASB

God, help me to know that You alone are the guide to the tough times I am living through. I place my hand in Yours today and ask for Your strength and guidance.

When you are fresh out of answers

The question is asked many times in our Growing Through Divorce for Children workshop: "Why doesn't my daddy (or mommy) want to see me and spend time with me anymore?" The question embodies the heartrending plea of a child to share time and love with a parent living through divorce. For reasons known or unknown, a parent who is going through divorce often pulls the plug from a relationship with a child.

Rejection is never easy to take, no matter how young or old you are. When we are rejected, we want to know what is wrong with *us*. We would do better to ask what is wrong with *them*.

It's tough to be a single parent after divorce. It is even tougher to try to answer all the questions your children come up with. Sometimes you would rather make up answers than say, "I don't know."

I remember a single mom telling me that if she had only one more prayer, she would ask God for wisdom. Today's verse from the wisdom of Solomon tells us that we have an open door to attaining the wisdom we need. All we have to do is be willing to listen to the Lord! That can be tough because most of us would rather talk than listen.

God speaks to us in many different ways. He speaks through the Scriptures, through other members of our Christian family, through prayer, and through the events of life. We need to focus on Him and listen for His direction. He may even give us answers to the questions our children ask.

"Come here and listen to me! I'll pour out the spirit of wisdom upon you, and make you wise."
—Proverbs 1:23
TLB

God, I need to listen to You today. I keep running in circles trying to find answers. Help me to be quiet before You and listen to You for the answers to my questions.

Give up or give over?

Every kid grows up with at least one tyrant in his life. I was no exception. My nemesis had a penchant for twisting my arm up my back until I yelled "uncle" about twenty times. I could never quite figure out what his ultimate goal was other than to make my life miserable and show off his superior arm strength. It was also my first experience in how to get relief from pain. Just yell "uncle" and the arm twisting would stop—until the next time.

Every week I meet people who want to throw in the towel and give up to their most recent life-twisting event. These people have one common cry: *Make my pain go away!* They echo the belief in our culture that says no one in today's world should be in pain.

To give up is to give in with no chance at winning. I know many divorced people who have chosen that pathway by letting their divorce beat them into submission with no chance for a new beginning. They continue to live, but they remain embattled and embittered by their experiences.

If you think you want to give up, let me suggest that you "give over" instead. The verse for today says that we are to give ourselves humbly to God. When we do that, He will lead us in the right direction for the growth and new opportunities we need.

Giving your life to God happens one day at a time. It is bringing God into every situation you face and turning that situation over to Him. When the going gets tough, you may still feel like giving up. That's human. But then remember, don't give up! Give over!

So give yourselves humbly to God. Resist the devil and he will flee from you.
—James 4:7
TLB

God, You know I have wanted to give up in so many areas of my life. It's hard to keep going some days. Help me give You my life each day and walk through it with Your guidance and support.

Winning over worry

How much time do you spend worrying each week? How many of the things you worried about were solved by your worrying?

If you quit worrying, what would you do with all the time you saved?

The only qualification you need to be a worrier is to be breathing. Dead people can't worry. Some psychologists say that 95 percent of what we worry about will never happen. That's a lot of wasted time.

Worriers live with a "what if" mentality. Everything they think about or do is followed by a question mark. They are controlled by imaginary events. Essentially, they live from a fear base rather than a faith base in life.

If you are a consummate worrier, you are probably raining on your own parade every day. The good news is there's a better way to live.

The apostle Paul told the early Christians (who had to worry about being killed for their faith) *not to worry about anything!* But he didn't just leave them with a command. He gave them instructions and told them to *pray about everything and thank God for the answers that followed.*

This is a powerful prescription for you if you are worrying your way through divorce today. Even though this struggle can give you a bagful of worries, God's word is clear: *Don't worry—pray!*

Today when you start to worry, tell God about your worries and trust Him to take charge.

Don't worry about anything; instead, pray about everything; tell God your needs and don't forget to thank him for his answers.
—Philippians 4:6
TLB

God, I spend too much time worrying. I know worry is interfering with Your plan for my life. Help me to give You my worries and experience Your peace.

When you are knocked down, reach out

Someone has said, "A person wrapped up in himself makes a small package." We all know a few people who are self-centered and want all the attention to be on them. We call them arrogant, haughty, proud, self-consumed. We usually think of them as kings, queens, celebrities, politicians, and such. We would probably never put divorced or divorcing men and women in that category.

I have met many men and women who have become totally self-focused and self-obsessed while struggling through divorce. They become so wrapped up in their grief and grumbling that they want everyone to cater to their wants and whims. They are all members of the Poor Me Club.

We all have a right to feel sorry for ourselves sometimes. We should reserve about 30 seconds each month to do that and then get on with our rebuilding process.

One of the best ways to get out of Pity City is to start helping others who are experiencing the same pain you are. Any effective recovery program is built on the "fellow struggler" concept. When you are knocked down, don't build a monument where you landed. Reach out and help others, and you will help yourself.

The best leaders in divorce recovery across America today are those who have been there themselves and are willing to reach out to others despite their own pain. If you have been feeling sorry for yourself lately, today might be a good day to start moving toward serving others who share your journey.

Do nothing out of selfish ambition or vain conceit, but in humility consider others better than yourselves. Each of you should look not only to your own interests, but also to the interests of others.
—Philippians 2:3–4 NIV

God, I have spent enough time feeling sorry for myself. Help me to start reaching out to others caught in the struggle to survive divorce. With Your help, I can help them and let them help me.

Divorce is no laughing matter

What kind of face did you see this morning when you looked in the mirror? If you are like most people in the morning, you probably didn't take the time to study your facial expression. If you are going through divorce, it probably isn't a happy one.

A happy face means a glad heart; a sad face means a breaking heart.
—Proverbs 15:13 TLB

Divorce is certainly no laughing matter. It is painful and depressing.

How do you put on a happy face when you have a breaking heart? It's not easy, that's for sure. It takes great energy to switch your emotions from sad to happy.

Putting on a happy face allows you to affirm your complete trust in God to guide you and direct you in everything. Your heart may take some time to catch up with your face, but as God works in your situation a glad heart will follow.

I have tried to help the many people who have gone through our workshops over the years by teaching them to laugh and smile at the many weird and bizarre things that occur in divorce. Some have told me they came in sad and went away glad.

God, put a smile on my face today that will reach all the way down to my heart.

Divorce is not a happy experience, but you can choose to smile more than you frown if you know who is guiding you each day.

Trash talking

Trash Talking. It's a term that came out of the NBA. It means that a player on one team harasses a player on the other team with mindless, in-your-face chatter in order to distract him from playing the game. Insults and profanity are the prime trash talking tools. When the final buzzer sounds, the insults end, and everyone goes off to dinner together.

Trash talking is a big part of divorce. Husbands and wives who once were madly in love with each other now can't say enough bad things about each other. Even the children are drawn into the conflict and are asked to choose sides. Divorce wars become word wars. Nothing is gained, and everyone is wounded.

There is a way to get out of this verbal jungle. Refuse to be a player in this game. There is a better use for your energies.

I am sure you are re-reading today's scripture and wondering if you stop criticizing your ex-spouse, will your ex-spouse stop criticizing you. Maybe, and maybe not. It does take fuel from both sides to keep the verbal fire raging. When one person decides to quit feeding the fire, the fire has a better chance of dying. Remember, scripture also says, "A gentle answer turns away wrath" (Prov. 15:1 TLB).

A critical spirit is usually followed around by a critical life. A critical life will be toxic to those it comes in contact with. We all fall into the trap of criticism from time to time. Just get out of the trap before it closes in on you.

God, give me a strong sense of self-worth so that someone else's criticism doesn't destroy me. Release me from being a critical person and help me to treat others with love.

Letters to my lawyer

She came up at the end of a workshop and handed me a thick typewritten manuscript. She explained that this was her daily journal of her travels through divorce country over the past eighteen months. I noticed it was titled *Letters to My Lawyer*. When I gave her a questioning look, she said, "Well, I had to address it to someone."

When I finished reading her story several weeks later, I realized how important it was to record thoughts and feelings to measure one's growth. It became obvious to me that this woman had grown by leaps and bounds over eighteen months' time.

There is a time to talk and a time to listen. There is also a time to talk and a time to write. Sometimes it takes more wisdom to hold one's tongue and engage one's pen.

This page is part of a book full of pages. Each page is taken from twenty years of experience with thousands of people journeying through divorce. It's my writing but their stories in many instances.

You have a journey and a story to share. It may never get to a bookstore shelf and only be told in snatches to friends over coffee or lunch. Nevertheless, I would encourage you to pick up a notebook and start recording your journey. It's good therapy, and it will help you measure your growth.

Much of what we read in scripture is the story of people's lives. Some are happy, others are sad. They are written for guidance, hope, and inspiration. Whatever attempt you make at your own journal may help others as well as yourself.

A wise man holds his tongue. Only a fool blurts out everything he knows; that only leads to sorrow and trouble.
—*Proverbs 10:14 TLB*

God, help me to learn that written thoughts are as important as verbal ones. Guide me in sharing my struggle and story so that others may be helped.

Discipline means I love you

I asked a sixteen-year-old a simple question: "How are things going at home?" His mom and dad were in the midst of a hotly contested divorce. His response took me by surprise. "They really don't care much about me or what I do. I guess they are in their own world."

My friend was not alone in what he was feeling. Thousands of young people are abandoned by their parents when the battles of divorce rage around them. Most of the time it is not by intent, but rather by neglect. Divorce can be so consuming for adults that they may leave the children to fend for themselves.

A parent's guilt over a divorce can also cause him or her to run in the opposite direction from the children. Whether it's from the fatigue of battle or the waves of guilt, children are often left with few rules and too little discipline as a result of divorce.

Discipline means I love you and care about you. I have told many parents to look their children in the eye during divorce and say "I love you" to them. It's hard to do because you might feel your child is thinking, *If you really love me, then stop this divorce from happening and wrecking my life and yours.*

Parenting doesn't stop during divorce. Standards and discipline should not be discontinued. It is easy for parents to get so overwhelmed by their struggles that they lose touch with the caring that keeps their children on track.

A word of advice: If your child ever says, "Don't tell me what to do. You couldn't keep your marriage together," smile and proclaim loudly, "Divorce has nothing to do with parenting. I am going to be your parent forever!"

Don't fail to correct your children; discipline won't hurt them! They won't die if you use a stick on them! Punishment will keep them out of hell.
—Proverbs 23:13–14 TLB

God, help me to show love to my children through discipline and correction. Give me the wisdom to reach out to them when they hurt and tell them I love them.

Putting failure behind you

How many things in your life have you failed at? Do you keep a list? Probably not on paper, but in your mind. What have you learned from failure? Not to fail again!

The LORD upholds all who fall, and raises up all who are bowed down.
—Psalm 145:14 NKJV

Many people give up trying to succeed at things because they fear what will happen to them if they fail. Instead of feeling free to fail and learn from the experience, they build a wall of fear around them that keeps them from risking and growing.

Divorce is the failure of a marriage, the failure of a relationship. The road to recovery starts when you can say, "The marriage failed, but *I* am not a failure!"

There are some common realities we all share regarding failure:

1. Everyone fails at something.

2. Failure is not a death sentence.

3. God is bigger than any failure in your life.

4. People don't want to be around other people who fail.

The message for us when we fail is that God sticks with us even if our friends desert us. If you spend time reading the Scriptures, you will find as many, if not more, stories about people who failed than stories about people who triumphed.

God, thank You for loving me through my failures. Help me to hang on to You when others are letting go of me.

The good news today is that God specializes in restoring people who fail.

Dream new dreams

We were talking about set- ting goals in a recent workshop. As we broke for our small group discussion, a woman came up to me and said, "I used to have goals, dreams, and plans for a future. My di- vorce has ruined that. Now I just hope to make it through each day."

Maybe you can identify with her. Divorce has a way of robbing you of your best dreams and replacing them with recurrent nightmares.

When old dreams die, you must replace them with new dreams. Even if your new dreams are smaller than your old ones, they still give meaning and purpose to life. When those little dreams are fulfilled, you can celebrate them as stepping-stones in your rebuilding process.

Here are a few good rules for dreaming:

1. Stop telling yourself it's too late.

2. Don't worry if everyone around you thinks your dreams are crazy.

3. Don't wait until everything falls into place before you start dreaming.

4. Write your dreams down, and build a plan for making them realities.

You must have faith to dream. The writer of He- brews tells us that faith is the "confident assurance that something we want is going to happen." If your faith is solely centered in *your* ability to make a dream come true, you will be in trouble. If your faith is centered in God's ability to make a dream come true, then you are on solid ground.

What dreams in your life can you commit to God today?

What is faith? It is the confident assurance that something we want is going to happen. It is the certainty that what we hope for is waiting for us, even though we cannot see it up ahead.
—Hebrews 11:1 TLB

God, help me to give birth to new dreams in my life, even though I can't quite imagine how they will come true.

A divorced person's prayer

Forgiveness is one of the toughest issues divorced people deal with. In our seminars, people always ask which night I will be speaking on forgiveness. I have learned over the years to keep it a secret because that is the night when everyone wants to be sick and stay at home.

We must practice forgiveness on a daily basis. We cannot live and build healthy relationships unless we forgive others. To live is to forgive. It is a tough challenge, because most of the time we consider ourselves recipients of unkind acts rather than perpetrators of them.

I have listened to many divorced people tell me of dastardly deeds their former spouse committed before the divorce. My feeling is that those bad things did happen, but that many times the perpetrator did not have a clue about what he or she was doing and the pain and hurt the acts would cause. We could call some of them random and thoughtless acts of unkindness.

It takes some people years to admit they made a mistake or injured another person. Some never face their mistakes. Because we are responsible only for ourselves, we cannot force anybody else to recognize their mistakes. All we can do is apologize and ask for forgiveness from those we have wronged and forgive those who have wronged us.

When Jesus was hanging on the cross, He forgave the ones who had crucified Him. Should we do any less?

"Father, forgive them, for they do not know what they do."
—Luke 23:34 NKJV

God, this forgiveness thing is tough stuff. Help me to follow Your lead in forgiving people who have hurt me. And help me to admit my mistakes and ask for forgiveness when I have hurt someone else.

Winners and losers

The cartoon caught my attention. The wife is walking out the door with two suitcases. Her husband stands in the open doorway clutching a letter in his hand. The caption reads, "Well, you may think I'm a loser, but I've got a letter here that says I may already be a winner!"

Who wins and who loses in a divorce? We could debate that question for a hundred years and never come up with a satisfying answer.

In a dysfunctional marriage, the spouse who leaves and breaks the chain could be considered the winner. In a marriage where one spouse has left the other to pursue another relationship, we could conclude that the person who has been left is the loser. My experience has taught me that there is more to lose in a divorce than there is to win.

The real question is not about who wins and who loses. The real question is what does a person do to move forward after the marriage has ended. Life doesn't end with a divorce. Divorce may send you off the freeway and down the road less traveled, but you are still alive.

The apostle Paul best summed up his own life by likening it to a race. Putting it in perspective, he said to forget about yesterday and focus on today. The final goal was still ahead.

Are you more worried about wins and losses than successfully running the race?

Brothers, I do not consider myself yet to have taken hold of it. But one thing I do: Forgetting what is behind and straining toward what is ahead, I press on toward the goal to win the prize for which God has called me heavenward in Christ Jesus.
—Philippians 3:13–14 NIV

God, most days I feel I've lost far more than I've won. Help me to focus my energies on running the race and being faithful to You.

Making a difference

In the midst of personal crises, we sometimes need to have one all-encompassing prayer that says it all from our hearts to the heart of God. The prayer of St. Francis of Assisi does just that. Will you pray it through several times today and let it affect your life?

For as many as are led by the Spirit of God, these are sons of God.
—Romans 8:14 NKJV

Lord, make me an
instrument of your peace!
Where there is hatred,
let me sow love;
where there is injury, pardon;
where there is doubt, faith;
where there is despair, hope;
where there is darkness, light;
and where there is sadness, joy.

O Divine Master,
grant that I may not
so much seek to be consoled
as to console;
to be understood
as to understand;
to be loved
as to love;
for it is in giving
that we receive;
it is in pardoning
that we are pardoned;
and it is in dying
that we are born to Eternal Life.

God, I know what the negative aspects of divorce are. With Your love and guidance, help me make a difference by working on the positive ones that give life.

Any man or woman going through divorce knows the experience is filled with hatred, injury, sadness, doubt, darkness, and despair. You can change those things and make a difference by not allowing them to rule your life. You can replace them with love, pardon, faith, hope, light, and joy.

Test the product

They come in little packages tied to your doorknob. They also come in your daily mail delivery. Some of them come neatly tucked into your Sunday newspaper. Others are handed to you as you enter the supermarket. What are they? Samples. Hundreds of samples of new products that their creators want you to test with the hope you will become a regular consumer.

How do you test the quality of your spiritual life? How do you know that your faith is strong enough to take you across the sea of divorce and land you safely on the other side?

The strength of our spirituality is made known in how we respond to the situations we encounter. We can fly into a panic and respond by yelling, threatening, throwing things, worrying, and causing mayhem in general. Or we can act as Jesus acted when things looked as if they were going out of control around Him.

The three things that marked Jesus' spirituality were tranquility, gentleness, and inner strength. Even when His life was threatened, He displayed those quiet characteristics that demonstrated His spiritual depth.

The world around us expects us to respond to adversity in a worldly manner. When we respond with inner spiritual strength, we portray what a Christian really is.

Your spirituality is tested in the tough times of your life. How is your testing process going?

Come and see what God has done, how awesome his works in man's behalf!
—*Psalms 66:5*
NIV

God, grant me that inner quiet and strength to know that in all the turbulence in my life, You are in charge and I can trust You.

All things are possible

The restaurant was crowded as I made my way to the cashier to pay my bill. Suddenly, above the roar of the breakfast crowd, I heard someone loudly calling my name. I finally spotted a woman waving her arms and running toward me. As she got closer, she said, "Remember me?" Not waiting for my answer, she informed me she was in one of my seminars a few years back, and she wanted to tell me how well she had done in rebuilding her life and career after her divorce.

I felt good as I listened to her success story. She thanked me for helping her get on track and for convincing her she could do the impossible.

Any successes that we attain in life start with a belief in our abilities. We are only limited by our doubts and the doubts that others have for us. If you think you can't, you won't. If you think you can, you can!

The good news today is that God believes in you even more than you believe in yourself. You are His unique, unrepeatable miracle. He has great plans for your life that are not dampened in the least by the experiences you have come through or are yet to go through.

If there is any fun in the difficult work I do, it is seeing people three or four years down the road from their divorce doing things they thought they could never do. New careers, college degrees, new houses, new friends, new lives.

God believes you can do the impossible because He supplies the strength for you to do it.

"If you can believe, all things are possible to him who believes."
—*Mark 9:23*
NKJV

God, help me to dream big dreams. When I attain them, help me to give You all the glory.

When you can't fix it

She sat in my office and cried intermittently throughout our conversation. Her frustration was etched on her face and on her heart. Like so many others I have talked with, she was having a hard time accepting that her husband was gone and involved with another woman. She said that she was not eating or sleeping and she could not concentrate at her job and probably should not be driving her car. She was an emotional basket case. She said over and over, "There must be something I can do to fix this marriage!"

You can never fix a marriage unless both partners want the same thing. It is hard to accept that reality if you are a person who always tries to fix everything.

When your world is falling apart and your mind is no longer in focus, it is hard to have a sense of peace and security. You want answers more than anything else, but what you need most is inner peace while you live through the conflict.

The scripture for today is not a Band-Aid for hurting people. It is an ongoing prescription that can help you adjust to any crisis in your life. All you are required to invest is your simple faith and trust in the Lord.

It is not God's desire to have His children consumed by problems they cannot resolve. It is His desire that you turn those problems over to Him and keep your hands off the problems. I know that is hard to do because your mind keeps resurrecting the turmoil and telling you there should be a way to fix it.

Peace can only come when you let go of things you cannot change and trust those things completely to God.

"He will keep in perfect peace all those who trust in him, whose thoughts turn often to the Lord!"
—Isaiah 26:3
TLB

God, my mind is scrambled. Help me to turn over to You right now the things that are out of my control but too often control my mind. Thank You for Your promise of peace in the middle of my war.

A year from today

Where do you plan to be mentally, spiritually, physically, and socially a year from today? Too far ahead you say? Then let's try six months, or even three months. One thing is for sure, if you don't have a dream and a plan to implement the dream, you will still be at the same place you are now, even two years down the road. That doesn't sound so bad if you are in a great place today and doing better than you expected. If you are doing poorly and are in a bad place today, however, that can sound like a death sentence.

Do you ever wonder why some people stay stuck, whereas other people move on down the road? They may be less talented than you, but they possess a wonderful determination to focus on the future as a way of moving through today.

Someone has said there are three things in life that constitute our happiness: someone to love, something to do, and something to look forward to. For some divorced people, that might look like three strikes and you are out. The person you loved is gone, the things you loved to do have lost their meaning, and there is nothing now to look forward to.

Each day we are faced with choices. Some are minor. Others are major and affect both our present and our future. We don't always make the right choices, but we *do* need to make some choices if tomorrow is going to be better than today.

Take a minute and write down some of your goals for your future. Post them on your refrigerator door and go to work on them.

So be truly glad! There is wonderful joy ahead, even though the going is rough for a while down here.
—1 Peter 1:6 TLB

God, I know my future is really in Your hands, but it is my present that consumes my thoughts. Help me to walk with You through today and live and plan for the joy ahead.

Of sticks and stones and bones

Remember when you were a kid and someone called you a bad name? You shrugged it off and said, "Sticks and stones may break my bones, but names will never hurt me." Wrong! If you had enough of those bad names tossed at you, they did hurt as much as broken bones.

Unkind names break your spirit, and if you are not careful they can mold you into their descriptive image. Take the word *klutz,* for example. If people call you a klutz, after a while you start thinking you are a klutz. When you drop something or do something you think is dumb, your nickname becomes an excuse for your actions.

The word *loser* has a similar impact. Many divorced people are called losers by people who apparently aren't divorced. If you accept what these people say and believe you really are a loser, you are dead in the water. Don't let other people's negativity influence your thoughts and actions.

Israel was called a loser by everyone outside Israel. Consequently, the people of Israel felt like losers, acted like losers, whined like losers, and lived like losers. But in God's eyes, they were His chosen people, and He certainly did not view them as losers. He saw them as winners and gave them new names to prove it.

How does God view you? The Scriptures tell us He loves us and calls us His children. He promises to give our lives meaning and purpose and will never leave us. He is our heavenly Father, and we belong to Him. So don't worry about what others call you. It is more important what God calls you!

Never again shall you be called "The God-forsaken Land" or the "Land that God Forgot." Your new name will be "The Land of God's Delight" and "The Bride," for the Lord delights in you and will claim you as his own.
—Isaiah 62:4 TLB

God, some days I feel like a loser when I would rather be a winner. Help me to know that no matter what others call me, You love me, and I'm one of Your children.

Run and pray

Be glad for all God is planning for you. Be patient in trouble, and prayerful always.
—*Romans 12:12 TLB*

We were about thirty minutes into the workshop when she came into the room. She was wearing a sweat suit and running shoes and had a towel wrapped around her neck.

It was apparent she had been running some distance before she arrived at the workshop. At lunch she came up to me and apologized for being late. She mentioned she had run to the workshop that morning. "How far did you run?" I asked. Her response caught me by surprise. "Seven miles," she replied. "And I plan to run seven more when I leave here today. I'm running right through my divorce!"

I am a runner, and I meet lots of other runners. I was really impressed when the woman told me that, prior to her divorce, she didn't even walk around her block. She said, "It was run or die."

I have shared that story with many divorced people. I don't know how many started running (or quit running) as a result. I do know that you and I are in better shape to handle things mentally if we take care of our physical bodies.

The apostle Paul often used running analogies in his letters to the early Christians. He compared life to running a race and winning a prize. He wanted Christians to know they were in the race, and he encouraged them to keep running their race for the Christian life.

I believe running and praying go together. Both involve endurance and the ability to hang in there when you feel like quitting. In today's scripture, Paul adds that when we rejoice in our hope, it will be easier to be patient in our pain, and both will be excellent preconditions for enduring prayer.

Both running and praying are hard work. They equip us to live each day more successfully. Maybe you need to hook them together in your life.

God, help me to take care of myself physically, as well as spiritually. Teach me the importance of good training so that I can honor You.

Setbacks are stepping-stones

It didn't come out the way his lawyer thought it would. He was trying to get sole custody and had a solid case to support his request. He had spent a pile of money in legal fees and was assured by his friends he would win. For some reason, however, the judge decided there would be shared custody. When I talked to him a few days later, he told me this was a colossal setback, and he wondered if he could live through it.

Jesus replied, "What is impossible with men is possible with God."
—Luke 18:27
NIV

In the land beyond divorce, as in the rest of the land, setbacks go with the territory. They can make us bitter, or we can try to learn from them and become better people. For most of us, setbacks are bitter pills to swallow, and we spend long hours trying to understand the big *Why?* I have learned, as did the father in this story, not to spend too much time and energy trying to answer impossible questions. Some things have no suitable answer in this life.

Setbacks, at best, can be teaching tools in our journey. They teach us how to live with strength and power when things don't go as we had planned. They also teach us to trust God more than we trust people. The trust that we place in others can bring us major disappointments. The trust that we place in God can overcome human betrayal, even though we will feel the pain.

God, help me to handle the things that don't work out as I planned. May I learn to trust all results to Your greater plan for my life today.

A positive way to handle your setbacks is to pray for God's guidance in all that you do. When the outcome is not what you prayed and hoped for, you can simply trust that God knows what's best for you. God may have bigger and better plans for you than you ever dreamed possible. Remember, the things that appear impossible for you are possible for God.

Who is the leader?

A crisis in leadership creates a crisis for followers. Joshua had such a crisis on his hands when he was 110 years old. After years of successfully leading Israel, Joshua had to face his people and ask them to choose between worshiping the gods of the Amorites or the Lord God. He told the people that he and his family would serve the Lord.

"But as for me and my household, we will serve the LORD."
—Joshua 24:15 NIV

Someone needs to be at the helm in single parent families today. Divorce often causes an abdication of leadership. It causes adults and children to sometimes become wanderers because no one takes a leadership role. I have watched some families become rudderless for long periods of time. Demands, schedules, and duties press on everyone, and everyone goes separate ways.

Single mothers often end up with primary custody, whereas fathers end up with visitation custody. Each expects the other to be the leader, and often neither takes the responsibility.

There are many forms of leadership in a home. The most important, from my perspective, is the role of spiritual leader. The scriptures designate the man for the role. What happens when that man is absent? Mom has to think about stepping up and accepting the challenge. Not easy, but desperately needed.

God, we have a lot of followers in this family, but we need a spiritual leader. Help me to take up that role today.

How are you doing in your home? Who is leading the family spiritually and setting the spiritual tone and direction for the family? It is not easy to do when you feel ill-equipped for the role. But remember, God can equip you as effectively as He equipped Joshua to lead Israel after Moses died. Ask for His help today.

Sing a new song

I wish I had a better singing voice so that I could sing out loud and not be self-conscious about it. I usually just hum or play the radio or listen to CDs. I believe music is one of God's most powerful communication tools. Through it we are inspired, challenged, encouraged, affirmed, and uplifted. In our moments of greatest pain and despair, God can give us a song and lift our spirits.

David the psalmist tells us to sing a new song celebrating what God has done. You might find that hard to digest in your life right now. There may be little to celebrate and less to sing about. If that is true for you, that's the best reason in the world to start singing, because it can lift you out of your valley and place you on a mountaintop.

What's that? You say you sing about as well as I do and you don't plan to do a concert in the park? Well, here's one of the best suggestions I can give you. Head down to your local Christian bookstore after work today and pick up some great praise-and-worship tapes or CDs. Listen to them at home. Listen to them when you are driving around in your car. Listen to them every chance you get, and I will guarantee that your spirits will be lifted. You may even find yourself singing along.

There is power in praise, and it can make the stuff you are plowing through seem pretty small, if not ridiculous. Praise music puts God out front in your life and puts a new song within your spirit.

Singing a new song is focusing on what God has done for you, what He is doing for you, and what He *will* do for you. It's time for a new song in your life!

Oh, sing to the LORD a new song! For He has done marvelous things.
—Psalm 98:1 NKJV

God, help me to dump the old songs of discouragement in my life and learn to sing new praises to You today.

Marathon love

You know the words from the marriage ceremony: *till death do us part.* It seals the marriage vow and says that only death can separate the couple from each other. You are probably thinking, *Yeah, right! Didn't work in my case. We should have used the words "till divorce do us part."*

The struggle with vows and promises is that we don't know what we are committing to until we have lived within that commitment for a time. It is easy to say "I will" before you are called to action. The words, *I love you,* are merely words until you realize that love is something you *do.* Love is never love until you give it away.

Human love often rides the tide of our feelings. When we feel good and things are going well, it is easy to love. When our world is falling apart and we feel miserable, our well of love goes dry. Human love has no long-term, enduring guarantee. I wish it did, because the world would be a happier place.

The good news is that God's love is *forever.* It is not conditional or based on feelings. That's why the Scriptures call God's love agape love. The word *agape* means "unconquerable benevolence." Love without limits. That's God's love for you.

The next time you feel unloved or betrayed by someone who claimed to love you, look in the mirror, smile, and say out loud, "God, thank You for loving me today, tomorrow, and forever."

Give thanks to the LORD, for he is good; his love endures forever.
—1 Chronicles 16:34 NIV

God, You are truly good, and I know that You love me when others don't. Help me to share Your love with someone today.

Peace for a troubled heart

After traveling hundreds of thousands of miles over the past seventeen years, I am about as familiar with airports as I am with the rooms in my own home. There are three things about airports that make them a lot like my home. They are filled with happy people, sad people, and people pursuing business. The happy people are going somewhere or are meeting someone coming to them. The sad people are leaving someone they love or are arriving to meet difficult situations. The businesspeople are just going about their business, often in a neutral gear. Homes and airports are places where the extremes of emotion are lived and expressed.

Leaving people you love is always hard. Divorce is a situation where partners leave one another. The loss affects everyone in the family.

Jesus understands what the loss of physical presence means. When He told the disciples of His impending absence, they became frustrated and fearful. The only way Jesus could ease those feelings was to promise the disciples that, even though His physical presence would be absent, the peace He would leave behind would be ever present. He further promised them that eventually they would be reunited with Him forever. The peace He left them with was only the equipment to live each day until they were reunited.

People you love can leave you and make life pretty stormy. God's promise to you in those storms is His peace. He will surround you with it because He loves you.

Peace I leave with you; my peace I give you. I do not give to you as the world gives. Do not let your hearts be troubled and do not be afraid.
—John 14:27
NIV

God, I pray that You will bring peace to my troubled heart today. Take away my fear, and help me to know that You are still in charge.

Winning back yourself

The group was standing by the door talking as I came into our seminar room. I only heard a few short comments, but what stuck with me for the evening was a question one of them asked: "Who won?"

Divorces divide people and possessions. The great legal battle often involves winning something. Houses, cars, boats, cabins, income, and savings are all up for grabs in a divorce. All the rules of fairness can go out the window.

I have asked many people over the years what they thought they won in their divorce settlement. Maybe the best answer I ever heard was, "the freedom to really be myself." That is extremely important if you lost your self-identity during your marriage. Some people lose their identity, whereas others have theirs stolen. The search to find it and reclaim it can take months or even years.

When all is said and done after a divorce, it is important that you get custody of yourself and realize that this is the best way to win what is most important.

Winning anything in this life cannot be compared to what we win when we have a personal relationship with Jesus Christ. Knowing God gives us a permanent victory over death and the promise of spending eternity with Him.

The good news today about winning and losing is good. In the end, God wins!

But thanks be to God! He gives us the victory through our Lord Jesus Christ.
—1 Corinthians 15:57 NIV

God, some days I feel like I lost everything. Help me to focus on things eternal rather than things material. Help me rebuild my life in positive and healthy ways.

Lift up your head

Have you ever watched people when they are walking? There are some who walk very erect, with head held high. There are others who seem to shuffle along with a carefree attitude. Still there are others who walk with their heads down, never seeing anything or anyone.

How do you walk? Head down? Head up? Sometimes the experiences we go through dictate our posture and demeanor. I have seen many people walking through life with bowed heads and hearts to match. They probably have a right to do so. They have had great sorrow and personal tragedy. Perhaps they are fearful of looking up lest something else fall on top of them. They might even want to place bags over their heads and claim anonymity.

King David went through a time of shame in his life. His head was so low that he probably bumped it on his knees. Yet even during his time of great depression, David still recognized that the Lord was his only hope.

Sometimes we fail to do as well as David. When we are going through a divorce, we may feel that there is little or no hope for us to draw on. We may feel that we don't deserve to raise our heads. But the fact is, you have a right to lift your head and to ask God when you get it there to keep it in place.

We can be thankful that God is in the business of straightening our heads, backs, and necks. He never intends for us to walk in shame. We are His children, His creative work. He loves us. We can walk through the tough places in life with head held high. How will you choose to walk today?

But Lord, you are my shield, my glory, and my only hope. You alone can lift my head, now bowed in shame.
—Psalms 3:3
TLB

God, I need Your help today to lift my head and heart. I can only do that through Your power. I have looked down long enough. Help me to look up!

Who's first?

Being first is important. People never remember who finishes in second or third place. Winners finish first and are always remembered.

Most of us always want to be first. That's where the power and the glory is. But there is one place in this life where that is not true.

In everything you do, put God first, and he will direct you and crown your efforts with success.
—Proverbs 3:6 TLB

The Christian life is the reverse of the secular life when it comes to being first. God's instructions are that we put Him first in our lives and put ourselves in second place. His directive is not just in a few things, but in everything.

We have a tendency to put God first only in the things that are of little or no consequence to us. In the important things, we place ourselves first. Perhaps this is why we fail so often. In times of crisis and loss, it is hard to sort things out well enough to know who or what is in first place in life. The urgent matters can take over, and God and His plan are often relegated to a miserable last place.

Why are we so hesitant to follow God's plan? Maybe we feel we can do it better or faster. The scriptures are full of stories of people who tried that route and failed. It was only when they put God first that His blessing was upon them and they were successful.

Today's scripture specifically tells us that there are great rewards for putting God in first place in all things. First, He promises that He will direct us. Second, He promises that His blessing will be on all our efforts. That's better than a money-back guarantee.

God, I think You have slipped out of first place in my life. Help me to put You back where You belong. I need Your guidance and direction today.

Who's first as you rebuild a career? Who's first in your daily schedule? Who's first in significant relationships in your life? Who's first as you walk the narrow trail through divorce country each day?

The search for a church

He told me he felt like a leper in his church. The people he shared life with when he was married now avoided contact with him. He sat alone in worship each week and wondered what he had done wrong. His wife was the one who had an affair and left him. Now it appeared that he was the one being punished. He said he was about ready to leave the church altogether.

I listened with compassion to his story and told him it was probably time for him to move on to a new fellowship of believers. I encouraged him not to give up on the Christian community as a whole because he needed love and encouragement.

It's an old story in many churches. We don't know how to be there for the people among us who are hurting. Even pastors and staff members are guilty of this neglect.

If you are divorced or divorcing, I have a few questions I want to ask you about your church:

1. Do you feel that your church family is judging or avoiding you?

2. Have you been asked not to serve in leadership positions in your church since your divorce?

3. Do you feel your church family reaching out to you and attempting to be a healing and loving community to you?

If you answered *Yes* to questions 1 and 2, then you are in the wrong church. You will grow better in a church family that provides you with the love and healing you need at this time in your life. If you answered *Yes* to question 3, you are in the right church. Accept the love and encouragement of your church family with gratitude.

Let us not give up meeting together, as some are in the habit of doing, but let us encourage one another—and all the more as you see the Day approaching.
—Hebrews 10:25 NIV

God, I want to be in a community of wounded healers. Help me to know if I am in the right place. If I'm not, lead me to that place.

The source of real power

I have found that there are two ways to do things: my way and God's way. I usually start out trying to do things God's way by praying "Thy will be done." But before long, I take it back out of God's hands and try to do it my way. Sound familiar?

I keep promising myself (and God) that I will stop trying to beat things into place in my life and learn to turn them over to God and let Him keep them. I need to pray and then rest in God, trusting Him to work out His plan in His time.

Author Glenn Clark says, "Our growth in power and happiness depends upon the number of seconds out of each twenty-four hours that we are resting in God." Like me, you are probably thinking, *That's why I am in trouble all the time.*

Most of us don't rest easily and let God's Spirit take over. For no apparent reason, God seems to do things on a totally different time schedule than we do. We get tired of waiting for the pieces to come together, so we race off to construct our own plans. I think God must smile knowingly every time we do that and wonder if we will ever let Him do things His way.

There is an old saying, "You can't push the river!" Rivers get to their destination by simply flowing along at their own speed. A friend of mine summed it up with these words: "Go with the flow, and use a light touch."

As you try to pick up the pieces and rebuild your life after divorce, are you willing to do it on God's timetable? The pushing, pulling, struggling, manipulating, and intimidating we use to try to speed up our lives only lead to exhaustion and despair. " 'Not by [your] might or by [your] power, but by *my* Spirit,' says the Lord."

So he said to me, "This is the word of the LORD to Zerubbabel: 'Not by might nor by power, but by my Spirit,' says the LORD Almighty."
—Zechariah 4:6 NIV

God, I have been trying to do things my way for too long. I want to give everything over to You and let You do things Your way.

Random acts of kindness

A group of grade school children were standing outside several of our downtown office buildings. Each child passed out long-stemmed carnations to the people beginning a new workday. Many of the workers asked the children what the carnations were for. The children replied, "It's just to say we care about *you*."

It was all part of a campaign called Random Acts of Kindness. The idea was to get people to be more loving and caring to each other for no special reason. If we could get everyone in a city of two million people to do one kind thing for someone else each day, this would be a better place to live.

Jesus tried to get a similar campaign going with His disciples. He asked them to take the love He had shown them and demonstrate that love to each other.

What would happen today if you and your family took Jesus' command more seriously? Many family members going through divorce do not feel loved any longer. If anything, they feel abused and cast aside. Every member could use a few random acts of kindness every day. Maybe someone needs a bouquet of flowers or a special love note placed on his or her pillow. There are many ways to say "I love you."

Are you willing to initiate a few gifts of love each day to those in your life?

A new commandment I give to you, that you love one another; as I have loved you, that you also love one another.
—John 13:34
NKJV

God, help me to reach out to those in my family who have been affected by this divorce. Help me do the little things that say "I love you" each day. Oh, and God, I almost forgot. It would be great if a few of those acts came my way.

When it's time to run to the fort

I remember sitting in the theater watching the old-time westerns when I was a kid. Every time the Indians came after the settlers, the settlers ran to the fort and barred the entrance gate.

A fort was a place of safety and refuge for early pioneers. It was usually run by the Army and was a safe haven from bad weather and enemy attacks. Its proud flag flying overhead said to one and all that there is help when you need it.

We live in a world that desperately needs more forts, places we can run to when the opposition is ominous and we are outnumbered by our problems.

Nahum was a prophet in a world filled with people who had problems. He told his people that they could run to the Lord when their troubles overwhelmed them. The Lord would be a stronghold and place of refuge and safety for them. The only thing they would have to bring with them was their trust in the Lord to take care of their problems.

It's the decade of the nineties, and God's commitment to you and to me has not changed. You might have enough divorce problems alone to fill your own fort to the brim. It doesn't matter how many or how few. You can bring them to the Lord with confidence that He will help you work them out.

Make a list of your ten biggest problems right now. Put them in an envelope and place them in the back of your Bible. Ask God to release you from your worry about them and increase your faith in Him to resolve them.

The LORD is good, a stronghold in the day of trouble; and He knows those who trust in Him.
—Nahum 1:7
NKJV

God, here's my list. You are my stronghold and fort. In faith I trust You with my problems for Your resolution.

The need for private prayer

I remember prayer meetings at my church when I was growing up. Sitting there without squirming was torture for me. It seemed the older people made the same speeches to God every week. There was not much variation, and I concluded that nothing much happened as a result of people's prayers.

A lot of years have gone by since those days. I can pray with others, and I can listen to them pray. I have found, however, that prayer for me is also a very private experience. I feel best when I can get by myself and pray to God.

The disciples asked Jesus how they should pray. In Jesus' rather long answer, He talked about privacy and promise of prayer. Jesus set a standard for quietly meeting with God in one's own room.

In prayer, you are talking with God and not the whole world. It is a one-on-one experience when your heart reaches out to the heart of God.

How are you doing with your private prayer time? You may need to lock the door to your room and wait until all the noise has settled down at night before you can meet quietly with God. Or you may need to get up earlier in the morning for quiet time alone with God. What is really important is that you do it!

But you, when you pray, go into your room, and when you have shut the door, pray to your Father who is in the secret place; and your Father who sees in secret will reward you openly.
—Matthew 6:6 NKJV

God, teach me about the privacy of prayer. Help me to set apart time and a place to bring my needs and concerns to You. Lord, also help me to listen for Your answers.

Downsizing

As if his divorce alone wasn't bad enough, Bob was informed that his company was downsizing and his ten-year tenure would come to an end in ninety days. He would be out the door with six months' severance pay and the option to connect with an outplacement agency to help him find new employment.

You may have lived Bob's story or may live it down the road. If you do, you learn one thing quickly: how to live with less.

When you go through a divorce, you are often downsized with no announcement and no job placement group to help you through the experience. I know of no other experience where you can lose so quickly what has taken you so long to acquire. Along with material loss, there is emotional, mental, physical, and spiritual loss. Adding up all your losses can make you realize that some of what you lost you really did not need anyway, and you may place greater value on what you have left and rebuild from there.

King Solomon (who was very rich) found out that possessing much can be a big burden. He learned that revering and honoring God was far more important than possessions.

I have listened to many people talk about what they lost in their divorce. Very few talk about what they have gained and how new priorities have come into their lives, along with new happiness in their hearts.

Divorce may have lightened your load in the material realm, but perhaps it has deepened your walk with God in the spiritual realm.

Better a little with reverence for God, than great treasure and trouble with it.
—Proverbs 15:16 TLB

God, people matter more than things. Help me to honor You with what I have and give no time to worrying about what I lost in my divorce.

Building inner strength

The cheerful voice on the other end of the phone said, "I just called to see how you are doing and to share how I am doing." Six years ago, this woman's voice did not sound cheerful. She came into our workshop a defeated person with two teenagers and a failed marriage. I think she cried more than she listened, and I wondered if she would survive the end of a twenty-one-year marriage.

On the phone, she excitedly talked about the birth of her first grandchild and her high school reunion. At the end of our conversation, she said, "It's been six years since I went through my divorce. I can't believe how well I've done and how far I've come in those six years."

Today you may feel like you don't have the strength or the desire to rebuild and renew your life. Most people feel like that after a divorce. Just know that others have been down the same path you are traveling now, and they have made positive changes in their lives.

I know my friend who called would lay claim to today's verse. She would be the first to tell you that she has come this far only by God's gift of inner strength. Without Him, she would still be at the starting gate.

You may have a long way to grow, but God will strengthen you from the inside out if you ask Him.

That He would grant you, according to the riches of His glory, to be strengthened with might through His Spirit in the inner man.
—Ephesians 3:16 NKJV

God, where will I be six years from today? I don't really know, but I do know that I can trust You for strength for the journey.

Every day is Thanksgiving

We have all participated in the annual Thanksgiving drama. A crowded dining room and a table set with enough food to feed an army. A brief prayer of thankfulness and on with the meal, followed by televised football and other assorted post-meal activities. At the end of the day, everyone ate too much and thanked too little.

In everything give thanks; for this is the will of God in Christ Jesus for you.
—1 Thessalonians 5:18 NKJV

Giving thanks on only one day a year is akin to tipping your hat to God in brief acknowledgment of everything He has done for you.

During divorce, you may feel you have little to give thanks for. Usually it takes something drastic, like a mission trip to a third world country, to make us realize the abundance we have and to appreciate it. Even that impact has a way of fading from view once we have been home for a few months.

I believe there is a healing quality connected to our act of thanking God for all we have. I believe we need to give thanks every day (and not just for the food we eat). Thanking God for what we have causes us to trust God to provide us with what we don't have. Thanking God for all we have also helps us realize that we are merely stewards of our possessions.

God, teach me to give thanks from a grateful heart for little and for much.

Look at your life for a moment and count your blessings, not your problems. Give thanks today for all God has entrusted to you.

Amazing grace

We stopped to talk for a minute in the mall. When I asked her how her divorce was going, she replied, "I am on a roll right now. Everything is going badly, and I just know it is going to get worse."

Does that sound like anyone you know? Somehow, when things get rolling in the wrong direction, they gather momentum and just keep rolling.

The scriptures don't focus much on the *whys* in life. They focus a great deal on the *hows*. When the apostle Paul was confronted with his own private angst in life, his thorn in the flesh, he told the early Christians that God gave him only one answer to his problem. The answer was not how to *escape*, but how to *survive*. God promised that He would surround Paul with His amazing grace, and that would help Paul to keep going.

Life spins a web of struggle around all of us sometimes. The non-Christian says run for your life and get out of the struggle. God says to the Christian, "My grace is sufficient for you, for My strength is made perfect in weakness."

Amazing grace is God's tender mercy applied to the toughest battles of our lives. For you today, that means God will come to you as you battle through divorce and supply you with more grace than you will ever need. You can trust Him.

And He said to me, "My grace is sufficient for you, for My strength is made perfect in weakness."
—2 Corinthians 12:9 NKJV

God, my struggles outweigh Your grace today because I have failed to trust in You. Help me to know that when I am weak, You will make me strong.

When you run out of words

Many divorced people are shunned by former friends who shared in their coupled world. From my experience, the main reason this happens is because married people don't know what to say to divorced people.

On the other hand, many divorced people don't know what to say to their married friends. As one man said recently, "I don't want to be around any married people. It only reminds me of what I don't have."

Words can hurt, and words can heal. Much of what goes on in divorce is a war of words. People inside the war, as well as people outside, search for the words to explain, console, and mend. Some days, you won't have any words at all.

Moses and God had a running dialogue in the early chapters of Exodus. God wanted Moses to be a leader, and He promised His help to Moses. Moses was afraid that he wouldn't know what to say when the opposition challenged him. God told Moses not to worry, He would tell Moses what he needed to say.

You know the rest of the story. God did what He promised to do for Moses, and He will do the same for you. As God gave Moses the right words at the right time, God can give you (and even your friends) the words that heal and keep friendships alive.

God, I need Your help in the communication area. Sometimes I just don't have the words I need to convey what I'm thinking or feeling. Please help me!

Avoiding tunnel vision

We were driving through one of those long tunnels in Colorado. Far in the distance we could see a tiny dot of light indicating the tunnel's end. For a minute I had a strange thought. What if that small exit was too small to drive our car through? We would be in that tunnel for a long time. I knew I was suffering from tunnel vision. From our distance, the exit looked smaller than it really was. As we approached it, it got lighter and larger.

We all have our bouts with tunnel vision when it comes to planning and moving toward the future. Many times we want to put our lives in reverse and go back where we came from because the future looks ominous and uncertain. Another option is to stay stuck in the middle of the tunnel.

What do you see down the road in your life? Options, opportunities, and growth? Or doubt, defeat, and despair? You might be thinking that you once had a vision for the future, but your former spouse ran off and took that vision with him or her. As true as that might be, you cannot quit moving toward tomorrow. Plan for your future; you have to live there someday.

Take a minute today and write down some of your visions for the future. Post them on your bathroom mirror so that you see them every day and begin to move toward them.

Where there is no vision, the people perish.
—Proverbs 29:18 KJV

God, help me get out of my tunnel and look toward tomorrow with faith and confidence in You.

Just call me peacemaker

She was in the middle of the aisle at the supermarket surrounded by five children who were all talking at the same time. They were arguing about what cereal to buy. As the volume grew louder, she finally pushed her cart ahead and said, "I'm tired of being the peacemaker in this family!"

All mothers should get a sheriff's badge when their first child is born. From that moment on, a part of their parenting will include being a peacemaker. Not an easy role, as both single and married parents will attest. One of the disadvantages to being a single parent is that you cannot threaten your children with, "Wait till your father (or mother) gets home."

Making peace and keeping it during a divorce is more a task for the sheriff's entire posse, and a few military regiments to boot. From my years of experience in this area, I would say that peace in divorce country is about as rare as finding gold nuggets in my backyard.

In His teaching of the beatitudes to the disciples, Jesus saw a world around Him that offered little peace and hope. He did not say run and hide from the currents of human need. He instructed His disciples to live in the midst of unrest and bring peace into it.

What are you really called to do and be in the midst of your divorce? I believe you are called to be a peacemaker. Do I have ten fast ways for you to do that? No. But I can suggest a starting point. Ask God how you can begin to be a peacemaker today.

Blessed are the peacemakers, for they shall be called sons of God.
—Matthew 5:9 NKJV

God, I don't fashion myself as much of a peacemaker, but with Your help, I am willing to try. Show me the little ways to start, and I will follow You.

Sure cure for sad spirits

Have you ever listened to a song that affected your life like a blow from a sledgehammer? It stopped you cold with its melody and message? It struck you with such force that tears came into your eyes and you were speechless? I am confident that we have all had those musically serendipitous moments when our hearts and souls were laid bare by music sent directly to us from the heart of God.

I believe that music not only lifts our spirits, but it can change our lives. It is often the tool that God uses when other things fail to reach us. It may well be the last thing that can catch our attention in times of unrest and conflict.

Like me and you, King Saul suffered at times from a spirit of distress. Today, we might call it depression. We don't know what caused Saul's depression, just as we don't always know what causes our depression. We do know that it happens, and if we don't find a way to deal with it, it will get worse and keep us out of commission in life.

I think I am a little like Saul. He was refreshed and became well when David played his harp for him. I always feel better when I can put a praise tape in my cassette player, dial out the world, and let the music minister to me. After twenty minutes of scripture set to song, my biggest worries seem to dissolve as I realize God is bigger than all the junk swirling around me.

A suggestion for beating the blues is to start your day with praise music. Play it when you get up. Listen to it in your car. Catch five minutes at lunch. Learn the words and sing to yourself. Music soothed Saul's distressed spirit. Chances are good that it can do the same for you.

And so it was, whenever the spirit from God was upon Saul, that David would take a harp and play it with his hand. Then Saul would become refreshed and well, and the distressing spirit would depart from him.
—1 Samuel 16:23 NKJV

God, help me let music lift my spirit each day and draw me closer to You.

The big squeeze

Did you ever feel like a thoroughly squeezed orange at the end of the day? The people in your life are still trying to squeeze another drop from you, but there is nothing left. As a friend of mine proclaimed, "I gave at the office, and I gave at the office, and I gave at the office. They took it all and asked for more. Now I'm out of gas and have nothing left to give."

Because of increasing financial demands in our world, many divorced men and women spend long hours on the job. When they drag themselves home they are greeted by more demands. They want to run and hide. Even weekends are filled with catch-up chores that never seem to get caught up. Few people I know are recharged and ready to go back to work on Monday morning.

How do you keep the world from taking all your juice and tossing you aside? In his letter to the Roman church, Paul offered some wisdom. He said the only way to deal with what is going on outside you is to develop inner strength that you can draw upon. That comes through allowing God to do some renewal and re-formation within you.

Some of the things that God does inside us are divine and mystical. We cannot explain them. God just does them. Others are practical, and we must work with them using our minds and our gifts. Reassessing our priorities is one of our practical responsibilities.

Remolding takes time. It doesn't happen overnight. But if you desire it in your heart and you seek God's guidance, it will happen. I know because I have been there!

Don't let the world around you squeeze you into its own mould, but let God re-make you so that your whole attitude of mind is changed. Thus you will prove in practice that the will of God is good, acceptable to him and perfect.
—Romans 12:2 JBP

God, I feel as if I've been squeezed a lot of the time. Begin some new work inside me that will help me attain a new balance in my life.

The plain truth

My mother had a way of getting to the truth wherever and whenever it concerned me. Whenever I tried to dodge the truth, my mother would say, "Just tell me the plain truth." I knew a little about lies and truth, but I could never figure out what the *plain* truth was all about. Maybe it was something like the plain vanilla we would order when all the other ice cream flavors were sold out.

There are many untruths in divorce. You have probably had some told about you, and you have probably told a few yourself. In an attempt to become an honorable person, we often try to dishonor the other person. A lot of that happens in the war between spouses. Sometimes the children are sucked into the battle of truth versus lies. After a while, everyone wonders how all this stuff got started and where it is going to eventually wind up.

David had done some lying in his life, and he soon discovered how God felt about it. In today's scripture, David makes a strong statement about truth. He tells us that God wants us to be honest from the inside out. Nothing hidden. Just tell it like it is.

If you were to ask me what I thought was one of the major sins in divorce, I would have to say *lying*. It is a national sport among many divorced and divorcing people. I know you can't stop someone else from lying, but you can stop yourself. You can change you, and that is the only person you are responsible for.

Behold, You desire truth in the inward parts, and in the hidden part You will make me to know wisdom.
—Psalm 51:6 NKJV

God, when I feel like a victim, I tend to wander from the truth. Help me learn to tell it like it is and know that when I do, I will be wiser and stronger.

A simple prayer

A news magazine show talked about the rise and fall of a Christian musician. As the camera was pushed toward one of the people involved, the interviewer asked, "How could you do this?" The response was, "I am just like everyone else. I am human and weak."

Have mercy on me, O LORD, for I am weak; O LORD, heal me, for my bones are troubled.
—Psalm 6:2 NKJV

What more can any of us say when we fail than "I am human and weak."

Marriages fail because men and women are human and weak. Businesses, societies, and nations fail for the same reason. That doesn't mean we are all doomed. It means that we are on a battlefield called life, and Satan would love to have us give up on our Christian life and just live any way we choose.

King David was recovering from personal failure when he wrote today's psalm. He admits what you and I already know: we are weak. He asked God to have mercy on him and to heal him.

Mercy means unmerited favor. You don't deserve it, but God in His love and forgiveness grants it when we ask. Mercy can be granted quicker than healing. Healing is a process. Mercy is an act.

David's road to recovery was much like yours or mine. In the midst of his pain, David asked God for help. That was all he could do, and that is all you and I can do.

God, have mercy on me, for I am weak. Heal me and grant me new life.

Get your mind on higher ground

Have you ever wished you could read the minds of the people around you? Have you ever wished the people around you could read your mind? I think it's safe to say that most of us would like to read other people's minds, but we want to have our own mind well hidden from public scrutiny.

We all spend a lot of time inside our minds thinking our thoughts and dreaming our dreams. It is hard to turn our minds off some nights, even when our bodies are begging for rest. A racing mind and a resting body are seldom compatible.

What do you spend your time thinking about? Getting even with your ex-spouse? How to pay the bills, find a job, discipline the kids, or find a new relationship?

Today's scripture sets a standard for muddled minds. Paul suggests that we focus on what God has planned for us as His reward for our faithfulness in following Him in this life. In other words, don't spend all your time looking around. Spend some of it looking forward to spending eternity with God, for that is the ultimate hope of the Christian.

Set your mind on things above, not on things on the earth.
—Colossians 3:2 NKJV

God, help me get my mind focused on You today and on Your promise to those who live for You.

From sorrow to joy to strength

When any healthy relationship ends, it is normal for grieving to begin. The length of the process depends on the person. For some people, the process ends abruptly, and they click into gear and go on with life. For others the process gnaws away at their lives for a long period of time. Grieving may start with an event, but it always ends up as a process. At some time in life, all of us will go through it.

Grieving is a mourning period where our sorrow outweighs our joy. It is a natural inclination for people to avoid sorrow and embrace joy. When our friends are sorrowful, we want to tell them to be happy, not sad. We want them to snap out of it. If the sorrow isn't yours, it's not easy to embrace it and identify with the person who is experiencing it.

In today's verse, Nehemiah tells the people to not stay in their sorrow, but to focus on the joy that belonging to God brings into their lives. He says that sorrow will be turned to joy and that joy will bring strength into their lives. To state it more simply, sorrow is a part of life, but you won't find any ultimate strength in it if you stay there.

Sometimes divorced people ask me when they will be happy again. I wish I knew. All I can say to them is, "Down the road a ways."

Healthy grieving is acknowledging why you are grieving and then allowing grief to go and joy to replace it. It takes time.

"Do not sorrow, for the joy of the LORD is your strength."
—Nehemiah 8:10 NKJV

God, You have said sorrow is for a season. I truly hope mine is a short one and that the joy You promise will help me grow stronger.

How do I get more faith?

"You are going to make it, Mary. You just need more faith."

"Good," Mary said. "Where and how do I get it?"

I am sure our group leader had good intentions when she told Mary she needed more faith. All of us need more faith *all* the time. We just wonder who's running a special on it this weekend. If we can find out, we will race right down there and buy some.

It takes a great amount of faith to believe you will someday live again in the land beyond divorce. Newly divorced people often doubt that will ever happen for them.

So how do you get more faith? Today's scripture says that faith comes by hearing the Word of God. I have learned that the more time I spend in the scriptures, the greater my faith grows. I read what God has done in other lives, and I gain strength from knowing that what He has done for others, He can and will do for me. I also read of how acts of faith were rewarded, and I gain courage to step out on my own feeble faith.

Do you want more faith? The scriptures are the fountain from which faith flows.

So then faith comes by hearing, and hearing by the word of God.
—Romans 10:17
NKJV

God, at best my faith is a little on the weak side. Help me to begin today to build it stronger in my life.

Deliver me from evil

He held a file folder with all his divorce papers under his arm as he talked to me. The longer he talked, the angrier he became. As his voice teetered on the edge of a scream, he slapped the file folder on my desk and said, "This stuff is a pack of lies! She is one evil woman!" He was referring to his former spouse.

My thought after he left my office was that he was probably right. If the allegations in his file were lies, his wife might well be an evil woman.

There is a lot of evil in many divorces—lies, allegations, untruths, accusations, and threats. You can be the kindest person on the planet prior to a divorce and end up angry and vindictive when the process is over.

How do you keep your sanity and spirit intact when evil is flying in your face? How do you keep a peaceful spirit in the combat zone?

There is a promise from God in today's scripture. You may need to write it down about one hundred times to get it in your head and heart. It promises that the Lord will deliver *you* from all evil. You will not only be brought through it, but you will also be preserved for what God has for you down the road. You will not be destroyed. You will be rescued. Knowing that, you can relax in the middle of any evil headed in your direction and trust God to take care of you. Don't worry about how God will take care of you. Just let God be God. Put a big smile on your face and refuse to be buried by the evil around you.

And the Lord will deliver me from every evil work and preserve me for His heavenly kingdom. To Him be glory forever and ever. Amen!
—2 Timothy 4:18
NKJV

God, I claim Your promise today in the midst of all I face. Surround me with Your love and care and protect me from harm.

125

What do you really need?

She grabbed his arm and dragged him toward the exit of the toy store. He kept pointing back down the aisle of toys and yelled at the top of his lungs, "But Mom, I *need* it!"

Every one of us has at one time or another echoed that little boy's cry when we looked at something we wanted to possess. If our compulsion is strong enough, we find a way to obtain the item, thinking that our need will be satisfied once the object belongs to us.

For most people, the possessions of life can be broken down into two categories: things we need and things we want. If you and I listed all our wants today, we might be writing for a while. If we listed just the basic needs to keep going in life, the list would be a great deal shorter. A roof over our heads, some food in the refrigerator, a change of clothing, air to breathe, and water to drink. That may sound like cutting to the basics, but most of us can survive well on a short list of things.

We all live through lean and needy times. Living through divorce can be one of the more critical times. The good news today is that we are not forgotten by God at the place of our need. God promises us that He will supply our needs, not our wants. You can trust Him today to do that for you.

For the needy shall not always be forgotten; the expectation of the poor shall not perish forever.
—Psalm 9:18 NKJV

God, help me to learn the difference between needs and wants and help me to live accordingly.

Ultimate freedom

I'll never forget the guy who came into our workshop one night proclaiming loudly to one and all that he was free at last. He wandered around the room in an exuberant manner, acting as if he had just won the Publisher's Clearing House sweepstakes. His award was simply that his divorce was final that day, and he was now free of his marriage.

About 25 percent of all the people getting a divorce feel like this man. The other 75 percent are distraught and confused and feel like this is the end of their lives. There is nothing for them to celebrate.

Freedom always has a price tag attached to it. The cost is *responsibility*. Many people want their freedom in divorce, but are unwilling to accept the responsibility that goes with it.

Back in the seventies, the cry of many was *Do your own thing*. It did not matter what you did, as long as you were happy. It was the Me Generation, but it never really brought any true freedom.

You can be freed from a dysfunctional spouse by a divorce, but your own personal responsibilities can increase a hundredfold. Freedom should have a sign attached to it that reads, *FRAGILE: Handle with Care*.

John the disciple recorded Jesus' words regarding freedom in today's verse. He tells us that real, true, ultimate freedom only comes in your life when you have a personal relationship with God. Any other form of freedom is merely an illusion and will, at best, be temporary.

Freedom comes in different packages. Has yours really come from knowing Christ?

Therefore if the Son makes you free, you shall be free indeed.
—John 8:36
NKJV

God, help me to understand that You are the only one who can give me true freedom.

127

Oh, what a beautiful morning!

I'm a morning person. I always have been. I like to get up early, run a few miles, and get ready for a new day. I usually hit the floor running when the alarm goes off. A new day symbolizes new challenges and new opportunities. It is a fresh start on the future, and if I had a good voice, I would race around my neighborhood singing, "Oh, what a beautiful morning . . ."

How do you face a new morning and a new day? Do you transfer all of yesterday's dilemmas into it? Add problems of the previous week, month, or year to your present load? I meet many people carrying their load of divorce baggage with them from day to day. It is hard to sing your way into a new day when your worries have sealed your spirit.

A Christian should be able to face each new day with joy and peace and be a part of a jubilant universe that celebrates its Creator.

Perhaps you should get up tomorrow and focus on the things you can be thankful for and rejoice in them. I think Isaiah knew something we are still learning. If you allow joy to fill your life, peace will be the by-product. If you are filled with peace, you will be quiet enough to hear the universe sing!

"For you shall go out with joy, and be led out with peace; the mountains and the hills shall break forth into singing before you, and all the trees of the field shall clap their hands."
—Isaiah 55:12 NKJV

God, help me to go out my door each day with a new joy in my heart. Help me to be willing to receive Your peace and hear the symphony of Your creation.

How will we make it?

If you have teenagers living in your house, you can smile at today's devotional verse. The two most important things to most teens are food and clothing.

I have counseled and talked with many single moms and dads who feel guilty when they can't meet the temporal needs of their children. They rage at the divorce and their former spouse for making them live in a setting of inadequacy. They also absorb the anger coming from children who don't understand why they can't have everything they want. It makes for some stressful living.

Today's scripture is not intended as a sermon to give your children so that they will stop eating and stop wearing the latest fashions. It is intended for *you,* so that your heart understands how God wants us to trust in Him for everything and learn His standard of value for the things we often worry too much about.

Many single parents wonder how they will make it when it comes to securing the basics in life. The answer is to trust that God will take care of you and your family.

The disciples struggled with the same questions and needs that we all have. Jesus' answer to them was that He understood their needs and would provide for them. He will do the same for you!

Then He said to His disciples, "Therefore I say to you, do not worry about your life, what you will eat; nor about the body, what you will put on. Life is more than food, and the body is more than clothing."
—Luke 12:22–23 NKJV

God, help me not to worry but to trust Your provision for my needs and the needs of my children. And God, not just today, but every day.

129

How to prevent a Maalox moment

I asked her how her divorce proceedings were going. She told me her husband had filed for bankruptcy, even though he had money hidden away around the world. Her fear was that he would get away with his masquerade, and she would be left without any money to live on after her divorce.

"You shall not steal, nor deal falsely, nor lie to one another."
—*Leviticus 19:11* NKJV

Does that story sound familiar? I hear different versions of it daily. Usually it's not millions that are being lied about, but only thousands. The end result is that one person ends up being a victim of lies and deceit, while the other person appears to be prosperous. The people I listen to are the victims. I never meet the victors.

One of the great dangers when you have this kind of number done on you is that you become hardened, calloused, and distrusting of the people close to you. You might even decide that you should take advantage of others before they take advantage of you. Some call that fighting fire with fire.

Principles for living a healthy life are found in the Ten Commandments and also in the book of Leviticus. Sometimes it may seem as if these principles were given to make our lives miserable, but in reality, they were given to make our lives whole, sane, and healthy.

God, help me not to fight fire with fire today, but to fight fire with love.

There are many schemes and lies that go along with divorce. A person in our town just published a book of dirty divorce games and how to play them. I am sure that many nice people ran out and bought the book so they could respond in kind to a former spouse's wickedness.

Your standard of behavior should not come from someone who is treating you badly. It must come from your own faith and belief system. You can avoid many Maalox moments if you choose to live by God's standards.

Tall tales and faithful spirits

It is hard to keep secrets, isn't it? We want others to know that we know something no one else is supposed to know. We also want them to know how very special we are because someone trusted us with their secret.

We often end up telling the secret and then asking the person we tell not to tell the secret to anyone else. Eventually everyone knows the secret, and there is no secret anymore.

How many times have you told your children, "Don't tell your father (or mother) what I just told you." Sometimes those secrets are aimed at injuring the other parent. The child is often caught in the middle when the other parent tries to find out what the child knows.

It is unfair to poison your children's minds against your former spouse. Children have a right to pursue a healthy relationship with each parent after divorce. Very often the secrets we tell our children about our ex-spouse are secret lies rather than secret truths. The lies often injure the children as well as the former spouse.

One of the ways you can end the cycle of secrets is to refuse to listen to them and refuse to pass them on if you do hear them. It would be helpful to teach your children to do the same.

Honesty and openness are rare commodities in divorce. But it only takes one person to initiate them and set new standards. Work on becoming a faithful spirit.

A talebearer reveals secrets, but he who is of a faithful spirit conceals a matter.
—Proverbs 11:13 NKJV

God, help me to learn to be honest, open, loving, and caring today. Help me not to play the game of secrets.

God is great and God is good

You recognize the title of today's devotion as the first words of a table grace we teach our children. In so doing, we are not just teaching our children words of thanks for the food, we are trying to teach them about a God who is great and a God who is good. The tough thing about that is that we are not sure we always believe that as adults.

When things are going great in your life, it is easy to give God the credit. When things are going poorly, we blame Him.

Is God only good in your life when good things are happening? Or is He good all the time because He is God, and the Scriptures proclaim His goodness?

Divorce is a bad thing that God did not cause. He also did not prevent it when you may have prayed that He would. He gives people the right to make choices, and some people make the wrong choices that others have to live with. God is still good even if you want to blame God for bad things that come into your life.

The prophet Nahum declared how he felt about God. After declaring God's goodness, Nahum added that God was a refuge or stronghold for his people when they struggled. He wanted God's people to know they were loved and would be protected from life's dangers.

Today, can you think of the ways that God has shown his goodness and protection in your life? Will you thank Him for that right now?

The LORD is good, a stronghold in the day of trouble; and He knows those who trust in Him.
—Nahum 1:7
NKJV

God, I need You to be a protective fortress in my life today. Help me to know that I am loved and Your goodness will be revealed as I trust You.

Good-bye to the lonely places

"If I could just stop feeling so lonesome, I could handle the rest of this divorce stuff," one woman said. With that, she threw up her arms in despair and headed out the door of the workshop room.

Behold, I am with you and will keep you wherever you go.
—Genesis 28:15 NKJV

I am sure she echoed the thoughts of many other men and women in the room. Divorce not only gives you hundreds of loose ends to resolve, it cuts you off from relationships that were once meaningful in your life. As people disappear from your life, you soon look up and discover you are very alone. Friends and family members who once filled the empty spaces in your life have pulled away, and you are forced to either reach out for new relationships or live in isolation.

Many divorced people expect others to reach out to them first, only to learn later that they have to do the reaching themselves and rebuild their communities. It is not an easy path to travel, but it is vital if you are going to grow through your divorce.

Today's promise was given to Jacob. He was starting a new segment of his life, and God wanted him to know that he was not alone in the challenges he faced. From square one, it would be God and Jacob. Others would come along later and add to Jacob's life.

God is with you today and urges you to say good-bye to the lonely places in your life. He is willing to walk with you as you reach out for a new community. Here is an affirmative prayer that can guide you and motivate you to reach out to others.

"Out of my lonely place, I came searching.
Out of my hidden fears, I came searching.
Out of my need for friends, I came searching.
Out of my quest for God, I came searching.
And I found a people who care, and a new love to share."
Thank You God!

Counting your blessings

The old hymn crept into the Sunday morning program of praise and worship songs we now sing. It seemed out of place at first amid all the new melodies and lyrics. Then, all of a sudden, it seemed to fit better than all the new music, because it echoed a lost theme in today's world. We seldom count our blessings anymore. Instead, we spend a great deal of time adding up our woes, criticisms, and complaints.

When you spend a couple of months or even years going through a divorce, you acquire a long list of assorted gripes. They range from your former spouse to your too-busy lawyer to your lack of money and resources. But all this griping won't make anything better. It will only increase your misery.

I want to propose a crazy idea to you today. Will you take a few minutes after you read this page and list the blessings that have come your way, even as you journey though divorce. You may have to think long and hard to come up with even a few, but I have known many people like you who have been surprised at the blessings they have found in the midst of their struggle with a divorce.

Today's scripture comes from David the psalmist, whose life was a roller coaster of chaos and blessing. In the midst of all the bad things he lived through, he still rejoiced at the things God had done for him. His focus was on the blessings rather than the conflicts and disappointments.

In a recent seminar, I overheard some attendees talking about the blessings in their divorces. They ranged from "I am finally free of conflict and negativity" to "Now I can make the choices I feel are right for my future."

Take a minute and count your blessings today.

The LORD has done great things for us, and we are glad.
—Psalm 126:3
NKJV

God, thank You for things great and small You have done in my life. You are faithful and I am glad!

On my way to tomorrow

How can you look forward to tomorrow, when you know it will be a repeat of today? That question was asked by a single mother of three who was part of the 38 percent of people in our country living below the poverty line. As I listened to her, I realized that I could not come up with an economic answer to resolve all of her financial woes. Our government doesn't even have an answer to that one.

For many single mothers and even a few dads, the economic picture in divorce country is often bleak and looks even bleaker in the future. Getting through each day is a major battle, and you know the same battle will be fought tomorrow and tomorrow and tomorrow.

Is there any kind of answer anywhere outside an economic one? I believe there is, but I believe it is on the spiritual front. Numerous scriptures tell us to bring our wants, needs, and concerns to God. It is a humbling thing to admit we don't have the answers and to ask for God's help in finding them. The things that are totally beyond us are never beyond God's ability to resolve.

We somehow enjoy hugging our problems to ourselves rather than turning them over to God. Our problem might be that we will have nothing to worry about any longer if we put God in charge of solving our struggles.

Today's verse comes from Jesus' practical message about life to His disciples. The disciples wondered how they would survive if they abandoned their vocations to follow Jesus. He kindly assured them that He would take care of their needs.

God can do that for you also. On your way to tomorrow, He can meet your needs today!

Therefore do not worry about tomorrow, for tomorrow will worry about its own things.
—Matthew 6:34 NKJV

God, I give You my economic needs today. I trust You to find Your answers to them.

God's question, my answer

May I take your order? Every waiter or waitress asks us that question when we are seated in a restaurant. The next time I'm in a restaurant, when the server asks for my order, I want to tell him, "One new car, one paid mortgage, one younger body, and the winning number for our state lottery."

Jesus asked him, "What do you want me to do for you?" "Lord, I want to see," he replied. —Luke 18:40–41 NIV

Most of us are either giving orders, taking orders, or filling orders. We are unaccustomed to any personal requests such as the question in today's scripture. Jesus asked the blind man what it was he wanted Jesus to do for him.

If Jesus asked *you* the same question today, how would you respond? Would you ask for a better job, house, car, or friends? Would you ask for things for your children? Would you ask for spiritual things? *What do you really want God to do for you today?*

The blind man answered simply, "I want to see." And Jesus restored the man's sight.

Sometimes we don't know what we want, and we don't know what we want to see. We may need to sort out our priorities and bring the important things to God in prayer. We may need to see ourselves more than anything else. With God's help today, we can do that.

God, help me to look inside myself and see me as You see me. Lord, I do want to see things more clearly in my life.

Can't wait for the season to change

It was warm and sunny at the bottom of the ski lift, as we dropped into our chair for a ride to the top of the mountain. It was early fall, and the leaves on the aspens were a bright gold. The lift attendant handed us a blanket, and we wondered what we would do with it on such a warm day. As we climbed toward the eleven thousand foot elevation at the top of the lift, we soon discovered why we needed a blanket. When we jumped off the lift, we saw patches of snow, and the temperature was in the mid-twenties. The season seemed to change in thirty minutes and from a few thousand feet. We couldn't wait to get back down to our car.

Seasonal changes in nature aren't quite that radical, but seasons do come and go. We measure our lives by them, and we notice that as we get older, they seem to pass more quickly. It is easy to wish our lives away by always wishing for one season to change into the next.

Like nature, we go through seasons of growth. Author Robert Veniga says there are seasons of sadness, anger, tranquility, and hope in all our lives. They don't follow any orderly pattern as do seasonal changes, but they appear instead in haphazard fashion and keep our emotions in a state of constant change.

Going through divorce can accelerate changes to warp speed. One day you're angry, the next day you're sad. You may wonder if these seasons will ever follow each other in a regular pattern.

The good news today is that God is in charge of the changes in nature and the emotional changes in our lives. He can bring order out of chaos and allow what we experience to change us for the better. We can seldom skip the tough seasons and enjoy only the good. We go through all of them to allow our change to be complete. God never leaves us quite like He finds us. We are changing and growing.

To everything there is a season.
—*Ecclesiastes 3:1 NKJV*

God, give me patience to live and grow through the tough seasons in my life.

137

New rules

The topic on the third week of our workshop is "How to Deal with Your Former Spouse." It is the segment that everyone waits for. (A few of our attendees think it should be entitled, "How to Make a Deal with Your Former Spouse.") It has become one of our more volatile and kinetic sessions over the past twenty years. The general feeling in the room is usually anger, and the general thought is usually of revenge. Hurt has a way of triggering the worst emotions in people.

The old rules for most people point to getting even. The new rules are found in today's scripture. James tells us to listen carefully, speak slowly, and not to get upset. If you follow these rules, you have less of a chance of getting your mind and emotions tied in knots. Yes, they are unconventional and fly in the face of what we would normally do when someone hurts us, rejects us, and replaces us. What these new rules mandate is that we treat war with a prescription of peace. Can it work for you? I believe it can, because God made these rules so that we could live in harmony with unharmonious people.

It is sad that many battles between former spouses go on year after year, and everyone loses in the process. If you are still playing by the old rules, today might be a good time to inaugurate the new ones from God's Word.

So then, my beloved brethren, let every man be swift to hear, slow to speak, slow to wrath.
—James 1:19
NKJV

God, it's time to dump the old rules and bring Your new ones into my life. Help me do that through Your strength, grace, and power.

Daily vitamins

We have lots of unused pills and vitamins around our house. The pills are leftovers from prescriptions that we no longer need. The vitamins . . . well, every time we hear about a new super miracle vitamin, we have to try it and see if we really will feel twenty-five years old again. Our motto seems to be, "If it doesn't work in three days, forget it."

We all tend to look for quick fixes in our lives. We do the same thing when our emotions are frayed. In place of long-term resolution, we demand miraculous, short-term cures.

There is no pill or vitamin that eases the pain of divorce. Ten seminars and sixty recovery groups may help, but one still has to walk through the process one day at a time for many months before healing becomes a reality.

I have discovered four things that can be real vitamins for rebuilding your life after divorce. They must come to each life through a personal request to God. Today's verse tells us to ask, and we will receive. Our part is the asking, God's part is the answering. The four things we need to ask God for are: Help me. Hear me. Hold me. Heal me. For twenty years, I have been hearing divorce recovery audiences ask for these four things.

These four petitions may well go beyond people in divorce and apply to everyone on the planet. We are all needy people. We need to be helped, heard, held, and healed, not just now and then, but on a regular basis. If those things do not happen, we shrivel up and die. Make them the important things you talk to God about on a daily basis. Your life will change if you do.

Until now you have asked nothing in My name. Ask, and you will receive, that your joy may be full.
—John 16:24
NKJV

God, this is my prayer today. Help me, hear me, hold me, heal me! Thank You!

Lord, change me!

How has divorce affected your life? Many of the people I talk to say they will never be the same again; divorce changed their lives forever.

Divorce brings many changes into a person's life, most of them unplanned for. Some changes make your life better. Some do not.

If divorce brings change by mandate, what changes would you bring into your life by your own choice? One way to cope with the changes brought on by divorce is to ask God to change you so you can meet your new situations. Very few of us pray for God to change *us*. We feel safer by asking God to change everyone and everything around us, while we stay the same. We might be fearful that God will change us, and we won't like the change.

God is not in the business of making people miserable. He desires the best for us, as He did for His Son. Jesus changed in the mental, social, physical, and spiritual areas of His life as He grew. We also need to change and grow in those areas as well. A commitment to change is a commitment to growth when our prayer is "Lord, change me!"

Is it time in your life for God to start changing you from the inside out?

And Jesus increased in wisdom and stature, and in favor with God and men.
—Luke 2:52
NKJV

Lord, as my circumstances change because of my divorce, change me so that I may meet the challenges that come my way.

Four bad words to get rid of

I have heard some highly descriptive terminology from divorced people over the last twenty years, but one woman's response to my question, "How are you?" really caught me by surprise. With a rather defiant look, the woman said, "Wounded, abandoned, unwanted, and worthless!" When I am caught off-guard, my tendency is to say something funny. But nothing funny came to mind when I heard her words.

This woman may have summed up how most men and women feel when going through divorce. You may feel that way today and wonder if you will ever feel any different.

Recovery in any area of life is learning to process feelings rather than to deny them. If you grew up being taught that certain feelings are wrong, you will feel strong guilt when you take ownership of those feelings. You will never recover from anything if you can't express your feelings and own them. You feel what you feel, not what others think you should feel.

It is easy to lose heart, mind, and spirit when your feelings are negative. Today's scripture offers solid hope. The apostle Paul says that our spirit is renewed daily by power of God, even when the exterior self is in pain.

We can authenticate our feelings today and know they are not a death sentence. As God works in us, those feelings will be replaced by the positive ones planted by God.

Therefore we do not lose heart. Even though our outward man is perishing, yet the inward man is being renewed day by day.
—2 Corinthians 4:16 NKJV

God, I have my own list of ugly descriptive words. I ask You to start changing them from the inside out in my life, today.

Ask for help

The voice on my phone said, "It took a lot of courage to make this call. I need help, now!"

As the man shared his story with me, I decided he was right. He did need help, and he did need it now. And it was hard for him to ask for help.

Many divorced people that I come in contact with echo that man's plea. Even in an age with helpful people listed in the yellow pages of every phone directory, many people are still reticent to ask for help. Some may feel it's a sign of weakness, while others may feel getting help is futile. Still others may be stifled with the shame of their experiences and not want others to know about their struggles. Many people in Christian communities want to hide their divorce from fellow Christians, lest they be criticized and judged.

It is pretty difficult, if not impossible, to go through your divorce without a support system and some wise counsel. Those who try it alone usually take a lot longer to navigate the rapids and may end up in the local psychiatric unit.

There are several people you need on your divorce support team. Family members are important even though divorce can splinter family groups. Your church pastor or even the pastor of another church can give you spiritual guidance. A local divorce support group can lend a great deal to your healing process. They are in every city across the country. Finally, a good family counselor is important if you need some special attention, as many people do. It goes without saying that a good lawyer is vital to your divorce.

That's your helping team. Lean on them. They are important to your recovery.

Where there is no counsel, the people fall; but in the multitude of counselors there is safety.
—Proverbs 11:14 NKJV

God, I need some help from other people. Lead me to the right people who can help me!

Yesterday's memories

She shook her fist defiantly as she described the way she had taken her form of revenge on her former spouse. "I burned every picture, slide, photograph, and video I had with him in it," she exclaimed loudly. "He is finally out of my life, and I won't have to deal with him anymore." She ended her outburst and walked toward her car in the parking lot.

Do not say, "Why were the former days better than these?" For you do not inquire wisely concerning this.
—Ecclesiastes 7:10 NKJV

I thought about her comments on my way home and wondered if this lady had found some unique way to obliterate her bad memories and to proceed to build happy ones.

Many divorced people would like to somehow put yesterday's grief and sadness out of their minds and vision forever. Because God has given all of us a memory in which we retain both good and bad, that is pretty hard to do.

For some divorcing people, the memories prior to divorce were good and the memories of the present are bad. One man recently framed this thought by telling me he had lost so much in his divorce that he could never regain it all if he lived for a hundred years.

Memories are hard to deal with. The good ones we reflect on time after time. The bad ones we want to bury so deeply that they will never reappear. What do you do with painful memories?

God, help me to sort my memories and file them away. Help me to learn from both the good ones and the bad ones.

I believe we file good and bad memories side by side in our lives. We have lived them both, and they are a vital part of what we are today. The only constructive thing we can do with either is learn from them and make some of the rest of our lives different.

God understands our journeys far better than we do. As He guides and moves in our lives, He equips us to put both yesterday and today in proper perspective and move forward knowing that He loves us and cares for us.

Kicking the fear habit

What's your biggest fear? That was my question to the seminar audience as we concluded our final session. They were to write their responses on cards, and I would tally the results later. On my plane flight home, I read their responses and was totally surprised to find that the number one fear in this group of people was the fear of never marrying again. The second fear was the fear of remarrying again.

Afraid to, afraid not to. That kind of fear can keep you living in a no growth zone for years, because fear paralyzes people and keeps them from healthy living.

There were assorted other fears also expressed in my brief survey. They ranged from the serious to the sublime, but for the respondents, they were all very real.

Divorce country is mined with fears. A big one is that you won't survive the experience and rebuild your life. Seeing those around you putting their lives back together is strong encouragement, but we need our own key that can unlock our fears and set us free.

Today's scripture presents that key as *love*. Simply stated, if we love God and know that God loves us, there really will be nothing to fear, because we know that God is in charge and will bring order and direction to our lives. He will not allow fear to put us on the sidelines. His love for us and our love for Him causes fear to disappear.

Take a minute today and make your own list of fears. Place it in the middle of your Bible and pray this prayer:

There is no fear in love. But perfect love drives out fear, because fear has to do with punishment. The man who fears is not made perfect in love.
—1 John 4:18 NIV

God, I give You all my fears. I love You and want to serve You. I know You love me and will care for me. May Your love grow larger than any fear I have today. Help me to know that Your love will always cause my fears to vanish.

Playing the shame game

"Shame on you!" We heard those three words after we had done something wrong when we were children. One of our parents probably said them, and we learned rather quickly they were not words of praise and affirmation. We realized we had done something that greatly disappointed our parents and somehow made them feel bad. We had shamed them, and now they wanted to put the shame back to punish us.

I meet men and women who are still wearing the coat of shame their parents outfitted them with forty or fifty years ago. It has become their permanent apparel as they roam through life.

The shame of divorce comes much later in life and usually involves the shame others direct at you and the shame you affix to yourself for the failure of your marriage. It is a quiet shame that is aimed at you emotionally.

When you load up with shame, your self-worth and self-esteem fly out the window, and you start planning your next pity party. Right after the party, you start to slide into a depression, and the black hole of despair becomes your permanent residence.

How do you deflect shame? Today's scripture gives us a start. When we allow God to go before us and be our shield, our glory, and our hope, only then can we lift our heads and allow the shame to vanish. He is not ashamed of us, so we have no reason to hang our heads.

If you are playing the shame game, today is a good day to give that struggle to the Lord.

But Lord, you are my shield, my glory, and my only hope. You alone can lift my head, now bowed in shame.
—Psalm 3:3
TLB

God, I guess we all feel ashamed at times. Please be the lifter of my head today.

Who's winning your race?

I was watching him out of the corner of my eye. He juggled his cellular phone in one hand, his daily calendar in the other, tried to maintain a conversation with two other men across the restaurant table, and jumped when his beeper went off. At the same time, he was attempting to eat his lunch. I wondered about the frenetic lifestyle that this man and many of us keep today. It's a big race, and only those who cross the finish line first will win the prize. We call it competition. Perhaps the correct term is chaos.

There are a million things to do each day when you are going through a divorce. The well-ordered life you had before divorce had two adults to make it work. Now there is just you, and you are not even close to the finish line. How do you keep up and get it all done?

Today's scripture tells us that God's ways are not man's ways. God has a whole different way of doing things and getting things done. If we can submit ourselves to God's way, we can move off the treadmill that we are on.

St. Vincent de Paul said, "He who is in a hurry delays the things of God." St. Vincent is telling you and me that God keeps a different time schedule and our hurrying only delays what God wants to do in our lives.

It may look like the swift and strong are going to run right over you, but if you can get on God's timetable today, you just might get a lot more accomplished.

Slow down today and give your schedule over to the Lord.

The race is not to the swift, nor the battle to the strong.
—Ecclesiastes 9:11 NKJV

God, get me off this treadmill, please. Help me to get on Your timetable today and every day from now on.

Watch your step

The hostess pointed down and said, "Watch your step," as she guided us to our table. I had eaten in this restaurant many times and the hostess said the same thing every time. I wondered what would happen if I did not watch my step. Perhaps I would fall down the three steps leading to the dining area and kill myself or just be maimed for life. Since I don't want that to happen, I follow instructions and watch where I am going.

How would you respond if someone told you to watch your step as you wander through the wasteland of divorce? Most people I know would say, "I'm watching, I'm watching."

The path through divorce is not usually well marked. Most people traveling on the path have never been there before and are fearful that they will lose their way and get totally lost. It's hard to read the signs along the way and follow their instructions. Most of the people I meet on this path don't even want to be there, and their resentment of walking down this path is strong.

Today's verse really speaks about following God's path and keeping our attention focused on Him. I believe God has a pathway through divorce for those who must walk there. Because there are many distractions on that pathway, He wants us to keep our eyes focused on Him and not on what is happening all around us. Our safety lies solely in sticking to His path and not taking side trips into our own desires.

It is not easy to stay in focus and stay on the right path when we are bombarded with distractions. St. Ignatius described our journey well when he said, "Act as though everything depended on you, but pray as though everything depended on God."

Look straight ahead; don't even turn your head to look. Watch your step. Stick to the path and be safe.
—Proverbs 4:25–26
TLB

God, keep me on Your pathway through this painful experience. Help me to watch my step and stay on Your path for my life.

147

A prisoner of denial

Have your ever had a bad dream and awakened frightened and believing that what you were dreaming about was really happening to you? We all do, and sometimes it takes more than a few minutes to shake the dream off and adjust to our present realities. Some of those dreams can be scary and very lifelike. Even a few days later we wonder if what we dreamed will come true.

Our dreams are mostly fantasy, and it is easy to deny them any significant foothold in our lives. What we live each day is our reality, and when we pretend our reality is a fantasy, we are on the road to denial.

Many people try to pretend that their divorce is not happening. They believe a departed spouse will one day return and life will go on again. I met one lady who had been divorced for four years. Her husband was remarried and lived in another state. Yet she assured me that he would return one day and they would go on as before. Only in her dreams!

Denial says that if you pretend something is not happening, then it won't be happening. Reality says that what is happening is really happening, and you need to make adjustments to live it in a healthy and sane way.

If you do not accept life's disappointments and crises and make a way through them, you can easily find yourself a prisoner of denial. God does not want us to be imprisoned anywhere. His desire is to heal us from our hurts and set us free to live. Anything less than that is not wholeness.

Are you stuck in denial in any area of your life? If you are, name your denial, and ask God to set you free to grow today.

"He has sent Me to heal the brokenhearted, to proclaim liberty to the captives."
—Isaiah 61:1 NKJV

God, help me to deal with my realities in a healthy way. Keep me from denial and help me to grow.

Focus on your rebuilding

Rebuilding your life in the months and years after divorce is closely akin to putting a jigsaw puzzle together without looking at the picture on the box. You might be able to put all the pieces on the table and turn them right side up, but fitting all the pieces together is an awesome challenge.

Real life and jigsaw puzzles have much in common. The pieces either fit or they don't.

There are four key pieces that form a foundation for rebuilding after divorce: the emotional piece, the relational piece, the practical piece, and the spiritual piece. Each piece is dependent on the other and should not stand alone. A good way to check any one of these pieces of your life is to ask yourself each week, "How am I doing in this area?" Ask your family and trusted friends how they feel you are doing in those areas. Sometimes we can lie to ourselves, but real friends will always tell us the truth.

Rebuilding takes time, focus, and energy. Today's scriptural directive tells us to work at the things of importance with all our strength. Halfhearted attempts will bring no lasting results. Today in our culture, casual and careless seem to define our attempts at growth and change. Real dedicated effort and long hours of hard work are seldom popular in a world looking for a quick fix for its ills.

Rebuilding is keeping track of your progress, setting new goals as you reach others, and always knowing you can expend just a little more effort. Being patient with yourself and allowing yourself a reasonable amount of time for growtn also is vital.

When you're assembling a jigsaw puzzle, you can't hurry the puzzle and force the pieces to fit. The same is true for your life.

Whatever your hand finds to do, do it with your might.
—Ecclesiastes 9:10 NKJV

God, rebuilding is slow. Help me to be patient and not push the process.

Peaceful enemies

I love you! I hate you! I'll get you!

Twenty years ago I wrote those words at the beginning of a chapter in *Growing Through Divorce*. The chapter addressed the topic of how to deal with one's former spouse on an ongoing basis. I am not sure that I really knew what I was saying then. I was just starting my twenty-year sojourn in the divorce field.

In 1994, those words are still perhaps the most descriptive of feelings between former spouses. Amicable divorces are rare. Most divorces are combat zones that can last for years and siphon money and energy from both parties.

Much of the time, post-divorce battles are fought by only one spouse who is bent on destroying the other at all costs. The noncombatant spouse is drawn into the fray unwillingly, and the divorce war escalates.

Is there another way to deal with this life-draining dilemma? Today's scripture sounds almost like wishful thinking. Does God's way really work? Is the prescription to please God with our ways the only way to bring a truce in the enemy camp? Yes, it is!

God's Word challenges us to put our energies and attention into learning to please Him in all our ways and to trust Him to take care of the war. It's a promise from God to you, and it will not work unless you do your part. I have seen peace come to some hopeless situations when one person gives up the battle and goes about following and pleasing God.

Today is a good day to walk away from the divorce war.

When a man's ways please the LORD, He makes even his enemies to be at peace with him.
—Proverbs 16:7 NKJV

God, I've been in the combat zone too long. Help me to please You and let You take care of my former spouse.

An angel in the furnace

Remember this story from Sunday school? As your teacher came to the climax, you wanted to yell, scream, and shout, "Yea Hebrew children!" The good guys won and showed a whole nation, and a king as well, who really had the might and power. But that happened a long time ago, and you were not there. Today you are sitting in your own fiery furnace wondering how to keep from being consumed. It's just you and the furnace. God may seem far away and preoccupied with others' needs right now.

Does God really send angels to help us when we are ready to become somebody's burnt sacrifice in life? Does God really care when the flames of stress and fear are licking at our heels? Does He really care about you today when you are discouraged and down?

I saw a bumper sticker that said what I believe is the answer to those questions. It read, *God cares!* It is a simple, yet profound statement of faith.

With the rediscovery and affirmation of operative angels in the past few years, we might do well to ask God once in a while to send one of his stronger ones to help us stave off the problems encountered in divorce. Yes, I'm serious! I believe God cares about you and me enough to send help when we need it. If the God you love, worship, and follow is the God of scripture, then He can do miraculous things in your life.

Remember though, God always does things His way and on His schedule. Your responsibility is to ask, wait, and be faithful while waiting for God to intercede.

"Look!" he answered, "I see four men loose, walking in the midst of the fire; and they are not hurt, and the form of the fourth is like the Son of God."
—Daniel 3:25
NKJV

Lord, help me to believe that You are still the God of angels and miracles. Stand with me when the flames of life are trying to do me in.

Reclaim your abilities

He stood in my doorway wringing his hands in total frustration. Finally he looked at me and said, "You know, I just can't do anything right anymore. Maybe I never could." My door closed, and he was gone into the night.

God has given each of us the ability to do certain things well.
—Romans 12:6
TLB

We all have those exasperating moments when we feel nothing is working out, and it's all our fault. Some men and women grow up in a family where they are repeatedly told they cannot do anything right. As they reach adulthood and build their own families, the litany of negativity from childhood has them well within its grasp. When divorce comes along, it only confirms one's feelings of inadequacy even more. Self-trust becomes a distant reality and self-doubt becomes a constant companion.

There are two ways to lift yourself out of self-doubt and restore your self-esteem. The first centers in today's promising affirmation from scripture. Notice this scripture does not say that God has given *some* of us the ability. It just says just *us*. That means all of us. You may be unaware of your abilities at this moment. You can discover them by asking God to help you claim and reclaim them. You definitely have some, and you can trust God to help you use them. The second lifter from the valley of self-doubt comes when your friends (and we hope family) see your emerging abilities clearly and affirm you in them. That may take a little longer than God's affirmation, but don't despair.

God, deliver me from the scripts others have written for my life. Help me to discover my unique abilities and use them well for Your glory.

Some of our best discoveries in life are made in the midst of a crisis. It can be a time of housecleaning and ridding ourselves of old tapes others have programmed into us. Reclaim the gifts, talents, and abilities God has given to you!

Where do divorced people belong?

She had been in one church most of her life, first as a single person, then as a married person, now as a divorced person. Her question was simple, yet disturbing: "Where do divorced people belong?" I wanted to smile at her and say, "Everywhere," but I knew in my heart what she was really asking. Her real question was, "Do divorced people belong *anywhere*?"

We all struggle with finding a place where we feel we belong. If we never find that place, we become tragic wanderers with no connection to life.

Divorce causes us to lose relationships we once had and valued. One belongs to a group of people more than to a physical place. When the people disappear, our place offers little comfort. If we don't rebuild our relational world after divorce, we will wonder if we really belong anywhere.

The anchor of all relational belonging is knowing with all our hearts that we belong to God. Today's scripture verifies that. People can push us away and reject us, but we can feel secure in knowing that we are God's people, and He provides His pasture for us as a place of security. I know that is hard to comprehend some days when what you really want is a crowd of people around you, laughing, loving, and caring for you in tangible ways. It is hard to walk a solitary path with just the knowledge that God loves you, and you will always belong to Him.

Divorced people belong to God, and God belongs to divorced people, no matter what the people around you think, feel, or say. Look up, smile, and say, "Thank you, Lord."

I can see clearly now

It was only a two-line verse, but its message was potent. It said: "Two men looked out from prison bars. One saw mud, one saw stars." It's the age-old war between pessimism and optimism. A glass half full or a glass half empty. Rain or sunshine. Happiness or sadness. Decline or growth.

What then shall we say to these things? If God is for us, who can be against us?
—Romans 8:31 NKJV

How did you view your life this morning when you woke up? If you are mired somewhere in the swamp of divorce, you probably found it hard to see the sun shining above. Your prayer going out the door to work might have been "Lord, help me survive another day."

Developing a positive, optimistic attitude in the midst of your struggles does not mean you are ducking from your realities and responsibilities. If your faith and trust is centered in God, it means He is in charge of everything, and you can base your positive spirit on that knowledge. Today's scripture sets a tone for the call to a new way of living if pessimism has overrun your life lately. It validates the little slogan, "God plus one is always a majority."

Many divorcing men and women feel that the clouds over their lives will never lift and the sun will never shine on them again. They allow the experience of divorce to dictate their lifestyles and control their futures. There is always the choice of sinking in your experience or rising above it. It takes God's kind of optimism to see things clearly. If God is for you, who is against you?

God, bring a new spirit of optimism into my life that is based on the simple truth that You are for me.

Life in the talk zone

If we hadn't turned out the lights, they might still be talking. It was almost ten o'clock, and all the other support groups had gone home. The later it got, the more it seemed these men and women talked. I got the feeling that if they quit talking, some bubble would burst, and they would find themselves back on earth.

I have discovered two kinds of people in our divorce recovery groups. Those who talk and talk and talk and those that seldom say a word all evening. Usually after a few weeks together in a small group, even the quiet ones start to talk. We try to keep the conversation centered on the questions our group leaders ask each night, but we have found over the years that most people want to talk about anything and everything they are feeling and processing in their divorce. Our designated questions usually fall by the wayside, as people need to vent their emotions.

One of God's great gifts to all of us is the ability to talk and to have someone to listen to us when we do. When we struggle, most of us want identification rather than answers. We want to know that someone out there feels like we do, thinks what we are thinking, and acts the way we are acting. Identification says I am not alone on this journey but have some kindred spirits that I can share my experiences with. I will support them, and they will support me.

When all the talking dies and we are alone again, we soon realize that along with our talking, we need God's power in our lives. Without God's operative power, all our talking can be just beating the air. After talking with our friends, we still need to talk to God and ask for His help in rebuilding our lives. His power is there for us to tap into each day.

For the kingdom of God is not a matter of talk but of power.
—1 Corinthians 4:20 NIV

God, thanks for friends I can share with. Please be the power center in my life today as I face my challenges.

A perfect picture

"We were the all-American family. Good kids, great community, wonderful house, good job, nice cars, great friends, involved in church and community, did everything together. Now we are the all-American disaster. How did our perfect picture get destroyed?" He started to cry as he finished his statement. I have heard stories like his many times in my years of divorce recovery work. They are all sad and painful and talk about the destruction of happy families.

Divorce is the result of shattered family pictures and dreams. There are many things that trigger the destruction. Affairs, job loss, alcoholism, drugs, vocational stress and burnout, and lack of communication, to name just a few. All can bring a deadly virus into a happy family and destroy it very quickly.

Picking up the pieces after a family has been destroyed isn't easy. Everyone is affected in different ways, and nothing will ever be as it once was. If I had not seen thousands of families rebuild after divorce, I would be as disillusioned as those who go through the experience. Many single parents I have known have worked long and hard to make their families work again and bring the lives of those involved back together. It takes hope, love, prayer, courage, determination, and hard work. But it can be done.

Don't spend too much time thinking about what isn't there. Thank God for what is there, and keep moving.

You shall rejoice in all the good things the LORD your God has given to you and your household.
—Deuteronomy 26:11 NIV

God, I thought we had a perfect picture and now it's changed. Help me to focus on the new one and rejoice in all the good things You give us.

Pull your children close

It was a long six weeks in the recovery group. All the problems were big ones, and I was exhausted on the last night. As I headed out the door, a woman came up to me with four children following behind her. She said, "Jim, I want you to meet my army. These are my children. Without them standing by me, I would never have made it through my divorce in one piece."

As I shook hands with each of her children, I was reminded again of the strength one can draw from his or her children in a divorce. The children were obviously proud of their mother's statement, and she was proud of each of them. They walked away, looking like a line of soldiers going back to battle.

One of biggest mistakes that divorcing people make is to shut their children out of their experiences. They forget that the children are going through the divorce also and have their own fears and needs. Most of all, they fail to realize the support parents and children can offer one another. It doesn't matter if the children are young or married with families of their own. Families are support systems and need to be called upon as such in difficult times.

Today's scripture speaks of a place of refuge for children. God and parents should supply that. The place of refuge is not so much a hiding place as it is a place of regrouping and reorganizing for what is ahead. Parents need a place of refuge, too. For both parents and children, God promises His care and protection.

Have you pulled your children close to you in your divorce? Or are they standing alone, as you stand alone? You need each other, and today is a good day to say that out loud.

He who fears the LORD has a secure fortress, and for his children it will be a refuge.
—*Proverbs 14:26 NIV*

God, battles are lonely when you don't have help. Help me to draw my children around me that we may support each other and draw strength from each other.

And the winner is . . .

Winning is certainly more fun than losing. Life conditions us all to want to be winners. Competition begins almost at birth and ends at death. Somewhere in between, we all want to win something, sometime, somewhere.

But thanks be to God, who gives us the victory through our Lord Jesus Christ.
—1 Corinthians 15:57 NKJV

I was asked a question on a radio show one day. The interviewer asked, "Who wins in most divorces?" My answer came quickly: "The lawyers. They get the money, and everyone else gets the problem of divorce to live out."

A whole lot of money and even more effort are expended in divorce to see who can win. The prizes? Money, children, possessions, homes, child support, alimony. Long after the tangibles are won and lost, many men and women continue trying to win the verbal battles. Many go on for years, with little reward.

Are you exerting undue effort at winning something in your divorce that really isn't very important in the long run? There is a time to walk away and get on with your life. Real victory today can be found in the scripture. Real victory comes when we give our battles to the Lord and let Him fight for us. No that doesn't mean you give up your lawyer and what is rightly yours by law. It does mean that you quit the useless battles.

Lord, real victory comes from You. Keep me from trying to win hollow victories.

Give it some thought and prayer today.

How to prevent sleepless nights

There are many sleepless nights when you are going through a divorce. The three big robbers of rest are fear, worry, and anger. If you doubt that, just ask yourself what you are thinking about when you can't go to sleep.

I suggest you take a reality check about an hour before you head for bed. Ask yourself what you are fearful of and how likely it is that those fears will become a reality. Ask yourself what you are worrying about and whether your worrying will change anything. Are you angry about anything, and will that anger rob you of your rest?

Today's scripture is really God's prescription for sound sleep and healthy emotions. When we harbor things in our spirits, they fuel all the negative emotions within us and rob us of peace. And they give Satan a gigantic foothold in our lives to accelerate our problems further and push us toward an emotional breakdown. The more we allow things to pile up, the harder it is to find rest.

A friend of mine who has had a few sleepless nights in his time says he has found a sure cure for insomnia. He gets up, sits in his favorite chair, and reads from the book of Psalms. He notes in a journal what the scriptures say to him and how they apply to his middle-of-the-night concerns. Within an hour, he claims he is ready to go to sleep with a new peace and calm flowing through his spirit. You might try this the next time your racing mind is keeping you awake.

If you are angry, don't sin by nursing your grudge. Don't let the sun go down with you still angry—get over it quickly; for when you are angry you give a mighty foothold to the devil.
—Ephesians 4:26–27
TLB

God, I know Your Word brings the promise of calm and stability back into my life. Plant its seeds deep in my heart each day.

Walking on water is scary

She told me she hadn't been out of her house in the many weeks since her husband left her. When I asked why, she told me she was afraid to just go out and do things on her own. She had always relied on her husband to accompany her everywhere and take care of most things beyond the door of her home. Now that he was gone, she was fearful that she could not take responsibility for her life.

If a good marriage is sharing experiences and responsibilities, divorce is the opposite. It doubles your responsibilities and redefines your experiences. You quickly have to learn to get beyond your front door and become responsible for yourself and also for your children.

For many post-divorce women and men, it is like learning to walk on the water, as Peter did in today's scripture. It is also knowing that the God who calls you to venture out and walk on the water will keep you from sinking in it if your eye is always on Him.

My friend, Ben Johnson, says that water walking faith demands four things from the walker.

1. You must clearly identify your feelings so that you can act out of them.
2. You must overcome the obstacles you encounter in expressing your real self.
3. You must identify sources from which you can draw strength in rebuilding your life.
4. You must take the risks that are involved.

Those four things put you in the place of real responsibility and faith testing. No one else can do your water walking for you. New beginnings demand that you take personal action and learn to trust God as you move in new directions. Your confidence will build slowly, and you will find a new sense of adventure in your life.

And Peter got out of the boat, and walked on the water and came toward Jesus.
—Matthew 14:29
NASB

God, I know I can't walk on the water without getting wet. Give me the faith to take the first steps.

Guidance in a foreign land

The journey through divorce can be broken down into two basic components. The first part involves living through the divorce. The second involves living beyond the divorce. Each stage has a very different set of problems to be resolved. For most men and women, the first eighteen months is spent wondering if you will survive the experience and what kind of shape you will be in if you do survive. A turning point of sorts occurs, and you start the second part of your journey. That can last for the next eighteen months, eighteen years, or a lifetime.

While the first stage is critical to your survival, the second is critical to your future growth and personal rebuilding.

One of the questions asked most often is, "How do I know where to go from here, and once I know, how do I get there?" When you survive the initial stage of divorce, you quickly come to the realization that you do have a future after all, and you want to make wise and healthy decisions.

Today's scripture is a signpost for getting good directions. It speaks about daily guidance, not just guidance at critical times. It also suggests that you will receive the strength you need to keep moving one day at a time. Guidance and nourishment are the two basic requirements for any kind of journey in life. If we receive bad directions and have plenty of nourishment, we might end up feeling good but living in a bad place. If we receive good directions and have no source of nourishment, we will be in the right place but without the strength we need to be in that place.

Sound confusing? It's not. If we ask God for His guidance and receive His strength, we will have everything we need in the land beyond divorce.

The LORD will guide you continually, and satisfy your soul in drought, and strengthen your bones; you shall be like a watered garden, and like a spring of water, whose waters do not fail.
—Isaiah 58:11 NKJV

God, I want to live my life so that I honor You. Guide me and strengthen me today and every day as I move toward tomorrow.

The really good news

The three of them were huddled by a car in the parking lot. When I walked by, I heard them telling their divorce war stories. While I was still within earshot, one of them said, "You haven't heard anything yet. Now let me tell you the really bad news." As I closed my car door, I wondered how bad that person's bad news really was.

There is lots of bad news in divorce. We hear about it, and we talk about it. Bad news gets more coverage than good news. It sells newspapers and magazines. It gets on television and in movies. It is analyzed and examined to the point of boredom.

There is some good news I want to share with you today from the scriptures. You may have heard about it before, or you may have read it today for the first time. The good news is simple. God loves *you* and tells you that if you believe in Him, you will one day spend eternity with Him. No one besides Jesus ever made that kind of promise to you and to me. Human promises as you well know are easily broken. God's promises are enduring and permanent and can never be broken.

Do you believe that God loves you today just as you are? That may be hard when you view yourself as bits and pieces of a shattered dream. It doesn't matter to God. He looks upon you with love and desires that you know Him, love Him, follow Him, and spend eternity with Him. His Son, Jesus, died on a cross to make that possible for you.

God loves you today. That's really good news!

For God so loved the world that He gave His only begotten Son, that whoever believes in Him should not perish but have everlasting life.
—John 3:16
NKJV

God, thank You for loving me so much that You sent Your Son to die on a cross for me. I believe in You as my Savior and Lord today. Thank You for Your gift of eternal life.

Sure cure for hunger

A television news story showed American relief planes dropping food by parachute to thousands of refugees in Rwanda. For these starving people, life was tied to the end of a parachute. If they were to live, they had to have some of this food. It was both a happy scene and a sad one. The sad part was there would not be enough food for everyone. Many would still die of hunger.

Physical hunger is only one form of human hunger. Others hunger for relationships, love, and friendship. There is occupational hunger and spiritual hunger. For many people, any form of spiritual hunger comes in dead last to the many other forms. Simply defined, spiritual hunger is allowing God to fill the empty space in our hearts, minds, and spirits that He carved out in each of us when He made us. We all have it, and He is the only one who can fill it.

The discussion between Jesus and his disciples in today's scripture was all about human need. As in many prior discussions, the disciples were more concerned about physical needs than spiritual ones. Jesus tried to show them that the physical would be taken care of if the spiritual always had priority. He kept saying the same thing over and over, but somehow it never fully registered until their upper room experience.

Human needs tug and pull at us every day. Filling our spiritual emptiness is low on our priority list. We hustle from day to day, unaware that we are spiritually hungry until a crisis such as divorce invades our lives. Suddenly we discover we have no spiritual resources to equip us for this crisis.

If our problem is spiritual malnutrition, the only answer is to allow God to be our sure cure for hunger by coming to Him and believing in Him. I call that growing spiritually. It happens a day at a time when we commit to following God and Him alone.

And Jesus said to them, "I am the bread of life. He who comes to Me shall never hunger, and he who believes in Me shall never thirst."
—John 6:35 NKJV

God, I have some real needs spiritually. Help me to come to You daily and allow You to feed me.

Are you afraid of God?

I grew up in a very missionary minded church. Missionaries were always coming and going around our church. Mission conferences happened several times a year. Mission reports, mission offerings, mission commissioning services were a staple diet for me growing up. One day I was asked if I would give my life to serving God on a mission field. I remember thinking, *If I do this, God will send me some place in the world where I will be totally afraid, miserable, unwanted, and forever misplaced.* My fear was that if I followed God, I would be unhappy for the rest of my life. Today I know that is not true, but many people still believe it to be true.

I meet many divorced people who feel God is out to get them because of their divorce. They expect a post-divorce life of misery because they know God hates divorce. If they ever come to a moment of giving their post-divorce existence totally over to God, they believe that God will get them good and their worst nightmares will come true.

We can be fearful of many things, but God should not be one of them. God is not in the business of making people's lives miserable. People make their lives miserable by living apart from God.

If God were to come to us today as He did to the disciples by walking on the water, we would either be afraid, or we would applaud and say, "Awesome God!" He will come to us today, however, in quiet assuring ways and tell us we have nothing at all to fear if we trust in Him. It doesn't matter how big our obstacles are, what punishments we feel we might deserve, or how small the level of our faith is. He comes to us in love and kindness and has good plans for our lives.

Jesus still says today, "It is I; do not be afraid!"

But He said to them, "It is I; do not be afraid."
—John 6:20
NKJV

God, wipe out my fear of allowing You to be God in my life. Help me to know You dispense love, not fear.

Home-coming time

He said it wasn't his home-coming, but he and his three children were going back to where he grew up. His divorce had brought untold devastation into his life, and he felt he would better find renewal, rest, and recovery if he returned to his roots. He sold everything he could, packed his kids in the station wagon, and headed out on Interstate 10 for a two-thousand-mile drive home.

It's always a leading question after a divorce. To stay or move away? To leave bad memories and pursue good ones. To go home again, wounded and defeated, or stay and grit it out in the valley of dashed dreams. It's a tough question, and each person must weigh all the options for his or her children and the future.

Today's scriptural command comes from Jesus after he had healed a man. I imagine the man was off and running because he had good things to share. He was probably bursting with excitement at his new life filled with promise and hope. He had good reason to go home.

If you haven't already done it, I suggest that in the next six months, you think about going home and sharing the good things God has done in your life. Don't forget to share with your family and friends how much you feel God loves you and cares for you. (Yes, it's okay to share the struggles you have had also.)

"Go home to your friends, and tell them what great things the Lord has done for you, and how He has had compassion on you."
—Mark 5:19 NKJV

God, it's hard to think about going home when I feel defeated. Help me to know when going home would be important to my growth.

God's information highway

They call it the information highway. It's all about how to get all the information in the world right on your home computer screen. A computer, a modem, a phone line, and the knowledge of the universe is yours at the touch of a key. Where will it all lead? No one is really sure, but the information highway is leading up to your front door. It is revolutionizing our world and dramatically changing our lifestyles.

God is not to be outdone, for He is the source of all information and wisdom under the sun. He has a great information highway that equips us on how to live life. It is called the Bible, and it contains several wonderful tools that we can employ in getting God's wisdom and understanding into our lives.

First, the Bible contains principles for living the Christian life. Principles tell us how God wants things done. Second, the Bible gives instructions. They tell us what we need to do. Third, it contains promises. This is what God says He will do. Finally, it contains affirmations. This tells us how God responds when we do what He wants us to do. It's a pretty simple formula that you can employ every day when you read scripture. It won't take long to begin to see that God has a definite plan for your life. He wants you to live on His information highway and follow His road map for your life.

The wisest man that ever lived, King Solomon, tells us to get wisdom and understanding and listen to God's words and never forget them. This is how we live through the hard places in life. It is how you survive a divorce and rebuild your life. It is slowly learning to ask the question in every situation, "How does God want this done?"

"Get wisdom! Get understanding! Do not forget, nor turn away from the words of my mouth."
—Proverbs 4:5 NKJV

God, I could use a big dose of Your wisdom today. Help me to turn to Your Word for guidance every day.

Suffering from scattered attention

It's called *crazy time*. I heard that term a few years ago in a divorce support group. It was used to describe one person's daily junket through divorce with four children, two jobs, a clunker automobile, and a vindictive spouse. She quickly admitted that her biggest struggle was trying to keep her thoughts straight and not suffer from scattered attention so much of the time.

Anyone who has ever been through snatches of crazy time knows what she is talking about. Divorce is often described as a too little or a too much experience. To keep your balance you have to learn to laugh a lot. But the best thing to do to keep your balance is to connect to the Lord daily and seek His direction.

Committing your works to the Lord, as today's scripture instructs, is simply asking for God's help and leadership in the tasks that lie before you today and trusting that He will help you keep your thoughts together.

As I write these daily pages for you, I must commit each day's process to the Lord and ask Him to direct my thoughts, or I would have little to say of any great consequence. The same is true for you as you read them. Ask God to direct your day.

Commit your works to the LORD, and your thoughts will be established.
—Proverbs 16:3 NKJV

God, some days my thoughts have been a giant jumble. Help me to commit myself to You today and live with a mind at rest, knowing You are in charge.

The cycle of growth

"I hate change!" she said in a rather loud tone of voice. As I was wondering if I had pushed the idea of change too strongly in our discussion, she added, "I hate changes I can't control! In this divorce mess, I can't control anything."

Many of us would yell a loud *Amen* to her comment. I like to control my changes as you probably do. My frustration is that I can't control everything. In fact, the older I get, the less control I feel I have.

One of the positive changes we all can control to some degree is our personal growth. We decide if we want to grow and then make plans to fulfill that growth. It may mean starting a new and more challenging job, moving to another home, going back to school, building a new support system, or doing something really easy such as dieting (just joking).

Pastor James Ryle makes an interesting and challenging comment on growth. He says, "Healthy things grow. Growing things change. Changing things challenge us. Challenge causes us to trust God. Trust leads to obedience. Obedience makes us healthy. And healthy things grow." Right back where we started. If you want to be healthy and stay healthy, you had better get into the growth cycle.

One of the great pleas in the New Testament is for Christians to grow. Paul even stated it more strongly when he said "Grow up!" Today's scripture tells us one way to grow is in our knowledge of the Lord. When we do, that growth (spiritual) is woven throughout all the other growth tracks in our lives.

It is a challenge to grow when we feel like shriveling up and dying. God is up to that challenge.

But grow in the grace and knowledge of our Lord and Savior Jesus Christ. To Him be the glory both now and forever. Amen.
—2 Peter 3:18 NKJV

God, help me to know You better and live on the growing edge in my life.

The God of lonely places

There is no ultimate escape from loneliness in our lives. We all experience it at different times, in different places, and as we walk through different experiences. Not one of us is exempt, no matter what our age, sex, or life experience.

Does God understand our loneliness, and what does He want us to do about it?

In his thought-provoking book *Never Alone,* author Joseph Girzone says, "God does not create us to live in isolation. He created each of us incomplete, so we would need one another, so we could reach out and touch one another's lives." If this is indeed part of God's plan, the answer to our loneliness is found in reaching out to others. They are not responsible for our loneliness but are part of the solution for it.

I believe God is very close to us when we are mired in our isolation, but we are often unaware of it. Even Jacob was unaware of God's closeness to him at a lonely time in his life.

Reaching out to others is difficult because the seeds of rejection are always there. When rejection hits us, we burrow deeper into isolation and suffer even greater loneliness.

In his book, Girzone provides a prayer you can offer to God when you feel alone.

"Surely the LORD is in this place, and I did not know it."
—Genesis 28:16 NKJV

God, I'm here. I'm not asking for anything, God. I just want to be near You and open my heart to You. I need You, Lord, and I'm here at Your disposal. Whatever You want to do with me, Lord, I'm ready. I don't know what to say to You. I don't know what to ask You. I don't even understand what is important for me. Speak to me Lord, my heart is open to You. But, Lord, please don't leave me alone.

If you are going out, get dressed!

We all remember some of our moms' favorite sayings. One of my mom's favorites was, "If you are going outside, make sure you are dressed." Did Mom actually think I would ever go outside without my clothes on after the age of two? By the time I got to high school, I had finally realized that she wanted me to dress appropriately for the weather.

Put on the whole armor of God, that you may be able to stand against the wiles of the devil.
—Ephesians 6:11 NKJV

What do you think God would tell you to put on before you left your home everyday? Today's verse talks about putting on the armor of God. You might think God was more concerned about warfare than warm fare. God's armor to protect you is more of an inner armor than outer apparel. Breastplates, shields, and helmets are descriptive words. Righteousness, peace, faith, and the Word of God are the real inner weapons. If you start any day without them, you are a moving target for the opposition and may come home with more than just a wounded spirit.

When you go through a crisis like divorce, you can feel as if you are going into the world each day with nothing at all on your body. You can feel defenseless to every situation and every person you meet. You feel vulnerable.

God, I need Your garments today. Equip me to live and serve You.

God doesn't want you to face any day like that. His aim is to clothe you with His garments and send you out in His strength so that you will stand firm against the opposition. So start getting His clothes ready to wear each day. If you are going out, get dressed!

The missing father

The title of the book was to the point: *Daddy Doesn't Live Here Anymore.* The content was aimed at helping children of divorce survive without a father living in their home. But all the advice in the world does not replace a father (or a mother) who no longer lives daily with the children.

Some children go in search of a replacement for a father who is no longer a key player in their lives. A few project all their hopes and dreams onto a stepparent. Many children discover that the stepparent can't quite stay in step with their lives.

After working more than twenty years in the field of divorce recovery, I have learned that primary parents cannot be replaced. Even the bad ones. We get one set of parents in life. Tragically, one parent can cut his or her ties with a child and spend limited time or no time at all with the child.

How do you find a missing father? The apostle Paul reminded the early Christians of a promise that God made to King David. That promise affirms that God is our Father and we all are truly His sons and daughters.

It is important to let children know their heavenly Father is always available to them. He will never desert them. He will provide for His sons and daughters in ways we may never understand. In God's plan, children are never orphans and outcasts.

"I will be a Father to you, and you shall be My sons and daughters, says the LORD Almighty."
—2 Corinthians 6:18 NKJV

God, help me to teach my children that You love them and they really belong to You.

Go fly a kite!

Go fly a kite! Those were the words printed on the buttons at the kite store. I bought one, but I must confess I was a little afraid to wear it, because when you tell someone to go fly a kite you usually mean you don't want to be bothered with him, and you want him out of your face.

I bought my last kite when I was in Hawaii. I flew it on the beach with a bunch of kids. I was the oldest kid there that afternoon, and it didn't take long for me to realize I was a bit rusty at kite flying. The other kites were ascending, while mine was descending. As I left the kids and went back to my hotel room, I wished for a few moments that I was a kid again.

Kids have a certain innocence about them. They're not embarrassed to ask someone to teach them something they don't know, they run and play and know how to have fun, and they easily trust people. Do you think kids know something that we adults have forgotten?

One day Jesus took a little child aside and told the adults gathered around Him that unless they became as little children they would never get into the kingdom of heaven. What do *you* think Jesus meant by that?

There is a little child within all of us adults. Amid all your struggles in divorce, maybe you should find some time to let the child in you loose, and go fly a kite.

"Unless you turn to God from your sins and become as little children, you will never get into the Kingdom of Heaven."
—Matthew 18:3
TLB

God, help me recapture childlike faith in an adult world.

Learning to hang in there

When I asked my friend how he was doing, he said that he was still hanging in there. It is a pretty typical response. My friend, like many people, was trying to hold on and keep his emotional balance amid the mayhem of divorce.

Most of the significant changes in our lives grow out of our experiences in the awful war zones. It is here that we are tested, and we can develop the mental and emotional fiber to make us stronger persons. James said that the tests and trials of life produce patience in us. I know many of you are thinking, *I don't need patience, I need answers!* We all want quick answers, but God wants something more lasting for us: the patience that will allow Him to take over and bring answers that will last and endure through our future.

All of us need to learn that staying power and endurance only come when our faith is tested. God has promised to be our strength for the long haul.

My brethren, count it all joy when you fall into various trials, knowing that the testing of your faith produces patience.
—James 1:2–3
NKJV

God, help me to trust You for the long haul and know that You will provide me with lasting and enduring answers.

Hide-and-seek

When you were a child did you ever play hide-and-seek, and while you were hiding all of your friends went home? You might still be there today if your mother hadn't called you for dinner!

There are some days when you would like to hide away somewhere and never be found. You could hide away from all the demands on your time and energy.

We all need a place to hide once in a while. The psalmist tells us that our ultimate hiding place is in the Lord. When we run to Him, He will keep us out of trouble, give us the instructions we need, guide us along the best path for our lives, and monitor our progress. That's a gigantic reward for hiding out with the Lord.

Here's a suggestion for today. Find a place in your home that can be your hiding place with the Lord. Some nook or cranny off the beaten pathway where you can retreat and not be disturbed. The scriptures say for you to go to your closet to pray, so maybe you've got a big closet where you can hide!

It's a good idea to take a little time each day to hide away from all the stuff in everyday life and seek the Lord in solitude. Even though God goes with us into the mainstream, we still need a time apart to meet with Him privately.

You are my hiding place from every storm of life; you even keep me from getting into trouble! You surround me with songs of victory. I will instruct you (says the Lord) and guide you along the best pathway for your life; I will advise you and watch your progress.
—Psalm 32:7–8 TLB

God, when I feel like running away and hiding, teach me to run to You and listen to Your voice. I want to know what Your best pathway for my life is each day.

Never give up

If you were to spend the next ten minutes writing down a list of all your troubles, how long would the list be? Would it be longer than a list of your blessings? Somehow troubles come to mind quicker than blessings. I guess it is because troubles need solutions, whereas blessings only need recognition.

Divorce can bring big-time trouble into your life. It wrecks finances, confuses children, destroys security, and dissolves trust. A man at one of my workshops recently asked, "Why not just give up and quit?"

Then he answered his own question by saying, "Because I know that God won't give me any more problems than He knows I can handle." In other words, God trusts us with our list of troubles.

Hemingway said, "Life breaks us all sometimes, but some grow strong at the broken places."

The apostle Paul said, "When I am weak, then I am strong."

If we give up and quit working toward solutions to our problems, we will never grow as strong as God intends for us to be. And when we feel our strength waning, we know we can turn to God and receive strength from Him, the strength to go on in spite of the mountains of troubles before us.

We don't give up and quit because we know that God is in control of everything, and all we need to do is move forward in trust.

We are pressed on every side by troubles, but not crushed and broken. We are perplexed because we don't know why things happen as they do, but we don't give up and quit.
—*2 Corinthians 4:8 TLB*

God, some days I feel like I'm drowning in my troubles. Help me today to feel secure in knowing that Your life raft is underneath me, and I won't sink in the waters of despair and uncertainty.

Sidetracks in healing

He asked a simple question as he got up to leave my office: "How long is this divorce going to hurt, and when can I start dating again?"

Over the years, I have been asked those questions hundreds of times. The premise often is that the pain will go away if one can find a replacement for the spouse lost in divorce.

It takes two to three years for most people to process their divorce and rebuild their lives. During that time, the very last thing a person should do is to try to make the pain go away by getting involved in another relationship.

There will always be sidetracks when you are on the road to healing and wholeness. Another relationship is one of them, and perhaps the most dangerous one.

In scripture, Nehemiah was rebuilding real walls. It was his calling, goal, dream, and directive from God. He took it so seriously that he wouldn't even take a break to be with some friends (who, as it turned out, weren't friends at all). Nehemiah knew that his task was important and distractions would only demean his calling.

Rebuilding your life is like rebuilding a wall. Instead of block and mortar, however, your building materials are emotions, fears, and frustrations. If rebuilding after a divorce is important to you, don't let anything get in the way.

So I sent messengers to them, saying, "I am doing a great work, so that I cannot come down. Why should the work cease while I leave it and go down to you?"
—Nehemiah 6:3 NKJV

God, help me to quit interrupting my rebuilding process so I can fulfill the directive You have for my life.

Real tough love

It was almost the end of our third workshop. The topic was How to Deal with Your Former Spouse. My wrap-up line to the audience was, "Don't forget God loves you. And don't forget that God loves your former spouse just as much as He loves you."

If I had passed out rotten eggs and soggy tomatoes earlier in the evening, the audience would have started throwing them at me at that point. I think the audience believed that God loved them, but certainly not their former spouses. After all, isn't God fair? How can He love anyone who has treated us so badly.

Fortunately, God doesn't grade on the curve. His love is all-encompassing and all-inclusive. He even said He loves sinners! (Now that sounds more like your ex-spouse, doesn't it?)

Most of us divide people into two groups: those we love and those we don't love. We have our reasons for our feelings toward each group. Jesus knew something we are still trying to understand. He knew that even our enemies respond to love. Hating those who hate us only adds fuel to the fire. God's antidote for hatred is always love. It is the opposite of how our world operates.

It doesn't matter if your former spouse is your friend or your enemy, you are called to tough love. Real tough love.

"There is a saying, 'Love your friends and hate your enemies.' But I say: Love your enemies! Pray for those who persecute you!"
—Matthew 5:43–44 TLB

God, I am having a hard time loving my former spouse. Help me to pray for my ex-spouse until Your seeds of love take root in my heart.

177

A simple promise

When we start our six-week divorce recovery workshop, I ask each participant to briefly share why he or she came to the workshop. Some admit to being dragged there by friends, and others admit their need and say they came to find some answers. I will never forget the man who said very directly, "I came for healing!"

Time heals, and healing takes time. Healing is a process, not an event. That process can be slow and painful, and we cannot hire someone to do our healing for us.

Where do we find help for healing? From friends we trust and a God who loves us. From counselors and doctors. From books that we read. All these and more combine to form a healing force in our lives.

The great promise of healing to every hurting person today is from God. The One who created us in His image is also the One who repairs us when we are damaged. We are never abandoned when we hurt. God's desire is for wholeness for you and me.

A divorce will leave you with many scars. Healing turns those scars into merit badges of growth.

"For I am the LORD who heals you."
—Exodus 15:26 NKJV

God, You are the One who can heal me and make me whole. Bring around me those who can help in that process, and help me not to hurry Your process.

A family membership

I was signing up for a membership at the local YMCA. The desk clerk asked if I wanted a family membership or a single membership. I had to stop and think for a moment. I was a husband and a father. But my children weren't going to play racquetball with me each week. How could they when they live four hundred miles away. "Single membership," I said, as I wrote out the check for the fee.

Families take on many different forms in our world. We have our families of origin. We have our families from marriage. And if we are divorced, we have yet another family system—the single-parent family. Some single parents have told me they don't feel they are part of a family anymore after divorce. They feel like bits and pieces of a system that no longer exists.

I suggest that there is another kind of family. It is God's family, and all who have received Christ into their lives and acknowledged Him as Lord and Savior are members of that family. We can call it God's Forever Family.

Writing to the early church at Corinth, the apostle Paul defined what a follower of Christ is. A follower of Christ is one who has chucked the old ways of doing things and has decided to do things a new way—God's way!

God's family is one big family. Have you signed up for membership in God's family?

Therefore, if anyone is in Christ, he is a new creation; old things have passed away; behold, all things have become new.
—2 Corinthians 5:17 NKJV

God, I am not sure I belong to Your family. Today, I invite You into my life to make me a new person. Help me to follow You from this day on.

The divorce quilt

The newspaper headline captured my attention: "Quilter Fashions New Life from Pieces of Old." The article told the story of a divorced woman in Washington, D.C., who made a quilt with vivid "scenes" from her divorce and hung it in a store window for everyone to see. One graphic square portrayed a monster face with spiders and worms spilling out of its mouth. "He lies," read the embroidered caption. Needless to say, the creator has received a sea of comments, most of them positive.

He heals the brokenhearted and binds up their wounds.
—Psalm 147:3 NKJV

If you were to create your own divorce quilt, what would your scenes portray, and what would they mean to you? Would this kind of project bring healing and closure to your divorce experience? Would it allow you to let go of yesterday and reach out to the future with expectancy? Your skill may not be quilt making, but you can probably think up other ways to aid your divorce recovery. (No, I wasn't thinking about making a voodoo doll of your ex-spouse and celebrating with a pin-sticking party.)

Closure is difficult for everyone. We fear if we close the door that we might be making a big mistake that will haunt us for the rest of our lives. Life is a never-ending series of beginnings and endings, some sad, others joyful. There are no guarantees.

Closure is an attempt to finalize and seal memories and begin the serious work of healing a broken heart and a bruised spirit. There are many avenues a person can take toward closure. Find one that works for you.

And as you mentally work on your closure project, remember God's powerful promise in today's scripture. Let Him help you heal your broken heart and bind your wounds.

God, my life seems like a crazy patchwork quilt some days. Thank You for guiding me through the crazy times of beginnings and endings.

How does God do that?

And we know that in all things God works for the good of those who love him, who have been called according to his purpose.
—Romans 8:28 NIV

David Copperfield is one of the world's best magicians and masters of illusion. We watch him perform on television or in person and come away with one question: How does he do that? If we were to meet him after a performance and ask him that question, we know he would not tell us. If we knew how it happened, if we could explain it, it wouldn't be magic. We know there is an explanation. We just don't know what it is.

When we see things in life that we don't understand, we want someone to make sense of it for us. We want to know *why* and *how*. With their divorces a few years behind them, people tell me they now understand why they had to go through it. They readily admit that they would not be where they are today in their growth and development if they had not gone through the pain of divorce. When I tell newly divorced people that they will grow and change and make it through their experiences, they are skeptical because the journey is still ahead of them.

One of the great challenges of dealing with any kind of pain is to believe today's scripture, to know that all things will work out for good for those who love God and live according to His purpose. Most of us have little problem believing the truth of the verse, but we want to know *how* God is going to work in our lives. Like a magic act, we want an explanation so that we won't be surprised by any sudden twists and turns in the journey.

We can't know why and how God works. All we can do is trust Him and let Him bring something good out of something bad, like divorce.

God, help me to be farsighted in my divorce and trust You to bring good from it.

Home alone

"I know you can't help me, but let me tell you my problem anyway," she said. "I don't have any problem Monday through Friday, but when I hit Saturday and Sunday, I get depressed. How do I deal with the lack of a caring physical presence in my life?"

"I will not leave you orphans; I will come to you."
—John 14:18
NKJV

As she talked, I thought through my list of stock answers: Keep busy. Go out with friends. Get a pet, and so on. Somehow these answers did not seem strong enough for her tough question.

What do you do when someone you thought cared about you is no longer there when you get home at the end of the day or on the weekends? You wake up in the morning to the frightening reality that you are home alone. Even if you have children living at home, they cannot replace the physical presence of a husband or wife.

One man told me recently that his loneliness was worse now that his ex-wife had a new man in her life and he had no one. He said his feelings ranged from anger to sadness to self-pity.

God, I go through some pretty lonely times. Surround me with Your comforting presence today and every day.

There are no instant replacements for someone who is no longer in your life. You learn to live alone, even when it is not always comfortable. I know that the healthiest way to deal with loneliness is to reach out to others and widen your circle of friends. By reaching out, you may be helping someone else who feels just as lonely as you do.

Today's verse speaks to men and women who are left alone. God's promise is to be with us, even when we have no special person to share our days with. We are never home alone when God is at the center of our lives.

God understands hard things

I was trying to teach my grandson how to aim my air rifle so he could hit the empty pop cans we had lined up on the wall. I did everything I could for him except pull the trigger. To his dismay, he kept missing the pop cans. Finally he said, "This is too hard to do." With that, he handed me the air rifle and walked away looking defeated.

"There is nothing too hard for You."
—Jeremiah 32:17
NKJV

We have all echoed the words of my grandson more times than we can remember. At the tough places in life when our reservoirs have been tapped out, we scream, "This is too hard. I can't do it anymore!"

At this point, some of us really do give up and withdraw from life's playing field. Hope is replaced by bitterness, depression, anger, and fear.

We all face things that are hard for us, but giving up is never the answer. Instead, the answer is to give in to a God who loves us and cares for us. The prophet Jeremiah summed up his feelings about the God who never quits in these words: "Ah, Lord GOD! Behold, You have made the heavens and the earth by Your great power and outstretched arm. There is nothing too hard for You."

When we face hard tasks and we feel like we are running out of gas, it is at that point that God must become our filling station. We allow Him to take us through the tough places. God understands the places that are hard for us and wants us to know that those places are not hard for Him.

Divorce is a hard place, but it is not too hard for God to help you through it.

God, some days I feel everything is too hard for me. I just want to quit. Help me give those things to You and let You take care of them in Your time.

Accepting where you are

I had just finished speaking to a group of single adults. When I left the building, I thought someone was following me so I turned around only to hear the question, "Do you have a minute?" As I paused to listen, the woman talked about how much she wanted to remarry and how being single again was terrible and lonely for her. Then she said, "But I am learning to accept where I am and am trying to focus on serving the Lord during these new days in singles country."

She echoed the feeling of about half the men and women I meet who have become single again either by divorce or the death of a spouse. They find themselves in a place of great discomfort after many years of marriage. They miss the shared experience of marriage, yet they realize they cannot quickly manufacture a new experience. They are often very uncertain about what to do with their lives.

There are some positive, growth producing things that you can do with your time after divorce. As you wait for God's right person for your life, you can also wait for the Lord to lead you into a particular place of service or ministry. This is a far better way to use your extra time than to visit all two hundred singles groups in your town over the next year.

When you are giving to others, you take the focus off your own emptiness and frustrations. Ask your pastor where you can serve in the church. Call Christian groups in your town and volunteer some of your unfilled time. Pray about where God might use you, and ask Him to put something squarely in your path. Ask some friends to share a new challenge with you. Don't stay idle, get involved.

I wait for the LORD, my soul waits, and in His word I do hope.
—*Psalm 130:5 NKJV*

God, help me not to focus on my loss all the time. Help me to share my life with others who need what I have to offer.

184

Getting the dirt out

Divorce is a dirty business. A friend of mine says, "Divorce is when love turns to hate and the lawyers get revenge." The divorce process is usually filled with injustices, accusations, threats, lies, intimidations, and a whole host of other very nasty things. It is hard to believe that the two people involved were once deeply in love.

I have watched many good people get dragged through a divorce for so long that they became mean-spirited. They begin to fight fire with fire and end up beaten and annihilated by the experience.

It is hard not to use dirty tactics when the other person is using them and seems to be winning the battle. Our human nature wants to get back at that person.

Today's scripture is a challenge to anyone and everyone who is losing ground in a divorce battle by slinging their own mud. It is an invitation to keep your hands clean (and we might add your heart pure) and gain strength by using a different tactic than your opposition. If you are God's person today, you can ask yourself, "How would God handle this situation?" It won't take you very long to come up with an answer. God's ways are not man's ways, but they work so much more effectively in the long run.

As you work through your divorce, are you keeping your hands clean, or are you allowing someone else's dirt to get all over you and rob you of your honesty and integrity? Are you getting stronger as you move ahead or getting weaker? Claim today's verse as God's promise to you today.

And he who has clean hands will be stronger and stronger.
—Job 17:9
NKJV

God, help me keep my hands and my heart clean. Strengthen me each day.

Worry is for wimps

Ulcers, headaches, weight loss, and general physical attrition can often be traced to undue tension in your life. For many people, tension has a more common name—*worry!* The more unresolved issues build up in our lives, the faster our worry level climbs, until we can't even sleep through the night without intermittent worry.

"Therefore do not worry, saying, 'What shall we eat?' or 'What shall we drink?' or 'What shall we wear?'"
—Matthew 6:31 NKJV

Worry is often the end result of accumulated fears. Everyone has a few that gnaw at both body and spirit. Fears are often accelerated when one goes through a crisis such as divorce. There are so many unknowns in divorce. If you are a person who thrives on certainty, working with unknowns can start you worrying in a hurry.

One of the powerful messages of encouragement throughout the pages of scripture is for all of us to give up worrying and start trusting God to take care of things. There is absolutely and positively no reason to worry about anything if you believe that God is in control and has a definite plan for your life. If you don't believe that, you should be worrying.

Worry is basically our expression of distrust of God. It says God isn't big enough and powerful enough to take over our struggles. If God can't do anything, then we need to worry and try to do everything.

Worry is for wimps who have no trust in God to take care of every need, in His time and in His way.

We don't stop worry by snapping our fingers. We attack it one step at a time by giving God the things we worry about as we become aware of them. Once given to God, we leave them there.

God, I believe that You are in control of my life. I am tired of worrying. I give You today the things that are robbing me of my joy.

I am God's unique, unrepeatable miracle!

Self-affirmation is a hard thing to do for most of us. When we attempt it, it can sound like bragging. Even the scriptures tell us to be humble and gentle. It is far easier to put ourselves down than lift ourselves up. Caught in the throes of a divorce, most people I have known tend to put themselves so far down that no one can even find them anymore. Self-worth, self-esteem, and self-affirmation appear to have forever disappeared only to be replaced by self-doubt, self-recrimination, and self-guilt.

One of the toughest challenges is to separate the person in divorce from the experience of divorce. The experience can deflate you and drag you to the depths of despair quicker than anything I know. It can rob you of your identity and obliterate your self-confidence. Somewhere in the midst of battling the demons of divorce, you have say to yourself, "I am still God's unique, unrepeatable miracle!"

Today's scripture tells us how God reacted after He finished His creative work in making human beings. I don't know if He whispered or yelled His feelings. I do know He said, "This is good!" I believe He said the same thing when you were born, and He has never stopped saying it because you are still His creative work and no life crisis can ever change that.

To begin with, maybe you can just smile more because you know that God still loves you and believes in you as His child. Are you smiling?

Then God saw everything that He had made, and indeed it was very good.
—Genesis 1:31 NKJV

God, I thank You that I am still Your creative work and that You love me.

The best home builder in town

"Your home is to be sold, and the profits will be split between you." With those words, the family court judge rapped his gavel and said, "Next case." Mary's eyes filled with tears as she realized her home of twenty-four years was being sold, and she would have to find a new place to live. It was the home where she raised four children and had many years of happy memories. Now, with the rap of a gavel, it would become someone else's home.

Mary's story is repeated thousands of times in courthouses across America. Few people are fortunate enough to keep living in their primary dwelling after divorce.

I have witnessed the tears of moving many times in the past twenty years. I can tell people it's a fresh start, or a new beginning, but it seldom eases the pain they feel.

How do you relocate, rebuild, and revamp your housing situation after divorce? Slowly, ever so slowly, and with the help of the Lord. Today's verse talks about allowing God to help you rebuild, even if it's in a one bedroom apartment next to the fire station.

New things and new places can acquire a feeling of comfort and belonging only over time. Just make sure that wherever your new residence is, you unpack when you move in. If you live out of suitcases and boxes, your new place will never feel like a home. Give God the opportunity to build you into your new residence.

Unless the LORD builds the house, they labor in vain who build it.
—Psalm 127:1 NKJV

God, I give You this dwelling to form around me as a place of starting over in my life. I want You to build it step by step and make me feel eventually that I belong here.

About seeds, tears, and joys

I grew up on a fruit farm as a child. About the only thing I really enjoyed about that experience was eating fresh fruit all summer long. I loved eating fresh cherries, peaches, plums, apples, grapes, and pears. I hated pruning fruit trees in the cold of winter. I hated plowing and hoeing weeds in the spring. I hated spraying the trees with insect repellent. I used to wish we could go from fruit season to more fruit season, and skip all the in-between work.

Growing things teaches you about seasons and processes. It also teaches you the responsibility of hard work if you are to savor the end result of growth and harvesting.

There are seasons to be experienced in divorce if you are to grow and your life is to move on. A time of shock, a time of adjustment, and a time of growth are three that are most typical. Combined together, the seasons of divorce add up to about eighteen to thirty-six months for most people. As in the seasons of nature, there are no shortcuts to growth. You have to go through the seasons and do the hard work to get to the growth rewards.

David the psalmist understood the growth process. He had planted his seeds, shed his tears, and reaped his joys. Many of his psalms reflect his experiences. David always took aim at the *joy* that was ahead of him. You can, too, when you realize that seeds, tears, and joys contribute to growth.

Those who sow in tears shall reap in joy.
—Psalm 126:5 NKJV

God, help me to know tears are a part of growth and some of the seeds I plant will be watered by them.

189

Hiding in a tree

I built a tree house in one of our big cherry trees when I was a child. Whenever life caved in on me or I just needed to be away from everyone else, I headed for my tree house. I can remember sitting there for long stretches of time, watching life go by about a quarter mile away. I dreamed, I thought, I planned, and I ate cherries in season. There are times today when I still wish I could run off to my tree house for a few hours.

When life launches a direct attack on all fronts, we all need some place to escape to for a time of regrouping. Many people don't have a place to go, and others don't feel that they need one. As today's world squeezes each of us a little more, we had better start finding our own little refuges and retreats.

The psalmist talks in today's scripture about God's hiding place and His protection. If God knows we need a hiding place and offers it to us, why are we so hesitant to admit our own need for it? Are we too busy, too proud, too important?

It is hard to escape the pressures of divorce without heading to the trees periodically. In those times and places of refuge, we can spend time with God, pray, think, journal, meditate, and regroup the loose strands of our life. Battle zones will always be there, but we can pick and choose our battles as well as our times of escape.

Maybe you need to start looking for a big tree!

You shall hide them in the secret place of Your presence from the plots of man; You shall keep them secretly in a pavilion from the strife of tongues.
—Psalm 31:20 NKJV

God, when life overwhelms me, hide me in Your secret place far from the battle zone.

Growing free

There is a rare gift that comes to those who have survived the ravages of divorce. Some talk about it openly, while others don't appear to understand it at all. Some fear it, others embrace it. It is a growing sense of individualism and freedom. It is being free to express your personhood in new and growing ways. Many people lived in dead marriages where their personhood was contained or stifled. It killed their spirit and they were often unaware that it had died.

Stand fast therefore in the liberty by which Christ has made us free.
—Galatians 5:1 NKJV

The freedom of personhood can be expressed in many healthy ways in post-divorce living. Let me share my eight favorite ways.

1. Don't let others ever put you in a box again.
2. Don't always be predictable. Make room for life's surprises.
3. Let what's on the inside of you shine through and show on the outside.
4. Learn to express your talents and gifts. Discover new ones.
5. Learn to stretch beyond your capacity. Welcome challenges.
6. Let those around you be who they are. Don't try to put them in boxes.
7. Thank God for the gift of being *you* every day.
8. Live and express your Christian life to the fullest.

That's really my short list. You can probably lengthen it with many things you can do to express your freedom of personhood.

The apostle Paul told the early Christians that Christ had made them free. They were never again to live under any form of bondage. Responsibilities came with that freedom as they do for you and me. Are you growing free in who you are today and in the freedom Christ offers to you?

God, thank You for the freedom I have in my life because of You. Help me to keep growing in that freedom and learn to express my personhood.

New and challenging

She said she wanted some new and exciting things in her life. When I asked her what those things were, she said, "You know, just new and exciting things." When I pushed further and asked her to name one new thing she wanted, she couldn't tell me. I think I know why.

For I'm going to do a brand new thing. See, I have already begun!
—Isaiah 43:19
TLB

We soon get bored with the routine, the mundane, the habitual things in our lives. We just know there must be something out there that would be new and exciting to us and light the fires of our existence and challenge us once again. We are uncertain what that might be, but we are certain it's out there somewhere.

Sometimes we affix a name to that something: new house, car, clothes, spouse, vacation, career, friends, city, state, or country, to name a few. We live under the false assumption that anything new can replace anything old and fill our lives with excitement. Many midlife crises that cause marriages to end are built upon the premise that something new will get us back on track in life. Many men and women find that after a few years of sampling the new, they want the old back again, but they find out it's too late.

The world of advertising doesn't hinder our desire for new things much. Advertisers want us to have everything new, and they assure us that when we do, we will be happy. Some of us have a number of idle things in our houses that we bought with the intention that our happiness factor would increase when we took them home.

God, people matter more than things, and You matter more than people. Help me to understand that and allow You to bring Your new things into my life.

What brand new thing would you like God to do in your life right now? Write it down. Are you willing to believe God will do something new in your life today?

Space for God

He was worn out after running four children through Saturday's Little League, choir practice, and Girl Scout garage sale. Then he had to do the grocery shopping and the laundry. When his best friend said, "See you in church tomorrow," it was little wonder he replied, "I'm not sure I have any room left for God right now."

"And surely I will be with you always, to the very end of the age."
—Matthew 28:20 NIV

Most of the single parents I know are in the same boat. Too little time and too many responsibilities. In the frantic whirl to keep up, God often gets the leftovers of a few tired hours on Sunday. Even taking the time to read this page today may make you wonder if you really can afford the few minutes you need to scan it. How do we find space for God in our frenetic daily schedules?

One positive way is to develop what I like to call "God awareness." That means I have the understanding that God walks with me through all the events of my life each day. It is consciously acknowledging that He is present with me everywhere I go. He is with me at the supermarket, in the board room, at the service station, at the children's activities, and on the freeway. When I know God is with me, I will know that I am standing on holy ground twenty-four hours a day.

God, be present in every moment of my life today. May I feel Your presence.

Too often we segment our lives and only consider church activities to be God's part. The rest we experience as our part, having little to do with God.

Brother Lawrence, in his book *The Practice of the Presence of God,* speaks of our being aware of God's presence in our lives every minute of every day. He wonders how any Christian can live a satisfied Christian life short of this goal.

When we allow God to be present daily in all we do, think, say, and feel, we won't be frustrated by giving God the leftovers. You can begin to do that today.

Where will I be tomorrow?

One of the biggest questions I am asked by people going through divorce is, "Where will I be a year from now?" Basically, what they really want to know is whether they will be in better or worse shape than they are now. They want someone to assure them that they are going to be fine. They want a little hope restored to their lives.

"For the LORD your God will be with you wherever you go."
—Joshua 1:9
NIV

One of my favorite prayers is by Thomas Merton. I want to share that with you today because it puts the question about tomorrow in perspective.

> My Lord God, I have no idea where I am going.
> I do not see the road ahead of me.
> I cannot know where it will end.
> Nor do I really know myself, and the fact that I think that
> I am following your will does not mean that I actually am doing so.
> But I believe that the desire to please you does in fact please you.
> And I hope I have that desire in all I am doing.
> I hope that I will never do anything apart from that desire.
> And I know that if I do this, you will lead me by the right road
> though I may know nothing about it.
> Therefore, I will trust you always
> though I may seem to be lost in the shadow of death.
> I will not fear for you are ever with me,
> and you will never leave me to face my perils alone.

Make this your daily prayer for the next seven days. It can change your life.

You are responsible for yourself

I meet many newly divorced people who are already anxious to remarry. Many are looking for persons who will take care of them so that they will not have to be responsible for themselves. This panic pushes many men and women into a second marriage prematurely, and that marriage also can end in divorce.

One of the goals in living beyond divorce is to become responsible for yourself. A part of that responsibility is setting goals that are attainable and will stretch your capabilities. Some of the goals we have people work on in our divorce recovery seminars are relational goals, personal goals, vocational goals, spiritual goals, financial goals, educational goals, family goals, and health goals.

A great way to set goals is to list your goals in a notebook. At the top of a page, write down the type of goals you will be listing (for instance, relational goals and personal goals). Underneath each heading list all the goals you would like to attain. Be sure to write the amount of time you will give yourself to attain that particular goal. This is not a project you spend a few minutes on and then abandon because it becomes overwhelming. Work on it a little each day as a discipline. As you attain each goal, record the date in your notebook.

Assuming responsibility for yourself is finding your own answers and not looking for someone to do your homework for you. After a period of time, you will find that you can really be responsible for yourself. You will no longer feel as if you have to find someone else to decide your future. You will find your own future with God's help and your patient day-to-day work.

Forgetting those things which are behind and reaching forward to those things which are ahead.
—Philippians 3:13 NKJV

God, help me set priorities and goals for my future and move toward them with Your guidance.

Making love tangible

A friend of mine asked me, "Have you been loved on lately?" I thought it was a strange question. I wasn't sure what he was asking. When I asked what he meant, he said, "Has anyone told you they loved you recently?" If I asked you that question today, how would you answer?

Divorce could be called the land where love got lost. Many divorced people search desperately for new love to fill the chasm left by a love that died. They soon realize that the love God shows them and the love that good friends share with them will have to substitute for the love they lost when their spouse left the marriage.

In his wonderful book *Happiness Is An Inside Job,* author John Powell says, "There are three kinds of love we are asked to give one another. They are kindness, encouragement and challenge. Only the mind and heart of love know when each is needed by the one loved."

When practiced, these three ingredients of love affect both the givers and receivers. They are action words that say, "show me how you will love me." Perhaps the most powerful of the three is encouragement. When we don't have loving encouragement, we dry up and quit believing in ourselves.

You can make love tangible today by sharing it in one of those three forms with someone you know who needs it. You can also be open to receiving it today.

Love never fails.
—1 Corinthians
13:8 NKJV

God, I know Your love never fails. Help me to put it into real-life terms today for another person.

God's way is the only way

Doing things God's way always starts with the process of waiting. This includes waiting *before* the Lord, spending time with Him listening for His guidance and direction. It also means waiting *for* the Lord to do things in His way and on His time schedule. It is simple to understand the process but hard to take action.

Today's scripture instructs us to wait patiently for the Lord to act. The reason we don't want to wait is provided in the second part of the verse. We might be afraid that while we are waiting, someone else might get ahead of us on the road to riches, success, fame, or whatever. My fear is that while I am waiting, others may be *doing,* and I will look silly and spiritually incompetent in comparison. Because we want to stay ahead of the competition, many of us hastily do something and seek God's blessing on it later. Before we take action we should ask ourselves, Is God in this?

As you face the questions and search for the answers after divorce, you will soon find that if you rest in the Lord and wait for His answers, you will save yourself a lot of heartache and turmoil. God will act in your life and answer your questions. Just wait!

Rest in the Lord; wait patiently for him to act. Don't be envious of evil men who prosper.
—Psalm 37:7
TLB

God, it seems I am always in a hurry. Help me to realize that things may move slower when I give them to You, but they will always come out better.

Get out of yourself

She started talking as soon as she got out of her car and didn't stop until she got back in it a few hours later. After three weeks, everyone in the workshop tried to avoid her when she approached them. Even her small group wanted her transferred to Alaska. The problem: she could not stop talking about her divorce war story. I'm sure some people in the room would have gladly paid her to stop talking.

She is not alone in her need to tell her story. Many do it to the point of self-obsession and never put yesterday behind them and move into today. If you choose to grow through your divorce, you will have to bring closure to it and move on with your life.

Getting out of yourself and refocusing your attention is not always easy. When you take the attention away from yourself, you have to place it on something else. I want to suggest several positive things you can do to refocus your attention and move on.

1. Begin to *listen* to both God and others around you.
2. Give others your full attention when they are talking to you. There is nothing worse than trying to communicate with someone who is tuned out.
3. Be willing to listen until you have heard everything the other person has to say.
4. Commit yourself to actively care for others through personal involvement and prayer support.
5. As you grow in spiritual sensitivity to others, ask God what He is trying to say to you in all your relationships. Listen for His answers.

Becoming a person for others will move you out of your own self-centeredness.

Serve the LORD with gladness; come before His presence with singing.
—Psalm 100:2 NKJV

God, help me to focus on the needs of those around me today and every day.

Who are your friends?

He was a leader in both church and community and had many friends. Six months into his divorce, his friends had all but abandoned him. His question to me was, "How can friendships of twenty years that run deep just disappear overnight? What can I do about it?"

One of the Pharisees asked Jesus to come to his home for lunch and Jesus accepted the invitation.
—Luke 7:36
TLB

The question is frequently asked because many men and women lose 75 to 80 percent of their friends while going through a divorce. I won't go into all of the reasons here, but I will suggest how you can rebuild a new community of friends.

All friendships fall into three categories: casual, close, and intimate. We need a broad sprinkling of each in our lives. The group of intimate friends usually is the smallest. It comprises the kind of friends who fit Dr. Stephen Johnson's description of closeness. Johnson says you can recognize intimate friends by listing the people in your circle who would fit the following descriptions.

1. Do you have at least one person nearby whom you can call on in times of personal distress?

2. Do you have several people you can visit, with little advance warning and without apology?

3. Do you have several people with whom you can share recreational activities?

4. Do you have people who will lend you money if you need it, or those who will care for you in practical ways if the need arises?

God, help me to keep my heart and arms open to the new friends You bring to me.

Were you able to put some names beside each question? Are they new friends or old friends? You may lose old friends after a divorce, but you can always reach out to new friends.

Will you pray for me?

Confess your trespasses to one another, and pray for one another, that you may be healed.
—James 5:16
NKJV

Picture the scene for a moment. It's Sunday morning and hundreds of people are streaming into your church. You are standing by the door and as each person passes, you shake his hand, introduce yourself, and ask, "Will you pray for me? I'm going through a divorce right now, and I really need the prayers and support of God's family." What would happen if you did that? They might call an usher and send you down the street to another church, or they might really do what you are asking.

It is hard to ask others to pray for us. We don't want to bother them with our personal problems, we want to believe we can take care of our own if we are strong enough spiritually, and we don't want them or us to feel bad if the answers we receive are not what they prayed for.

Asking others to pray for you is allowing yourself to become emotionally vulnerable to others. There is always a fear that what we share will be used against us in the form of gossip or judgment. It is easier to hide and just maintain our own lonely prayer vigil.

In today's scripture, James emphasized the "one another" principle. Most of us would run away at the mere thought of confessing anything in our life to a Christian friend. James says, "Confess and pray." I believe that our confession is a way to share our weaknesses, and when we share how weak we really are, we need to have others pray for us. The promise of this scripture is a simple one: you will be healed.

There is a time when you call your friends and say simply, "Pray for me. Right now!" It will take courage on your part, but once you do it, you will no longer feel alone.

God, asking for prayer is hard for me. Give me the courage to do it when I need to.

Stop, look, listen, and learn

The old saying goes like this: Those who don't learn from their experiences are doomed to repeat them. That can be scary when applied to life in general and even more scary when applied to a divorce experience. That's why we put such an emphasis on growth and time in our workshops. If recovery from divorce takes two to three years, the best use of that time is to learn all you can learn from where you have been and apply it to where you are headed. We have a short list of questions from our workshop that you can answer today.

So be truly glad! There is wonderful joy ahead, even though the going is rough for a while down here.
—1 Peter 1:6 TLB

1. What have you learned about your feelings?
2. What have you learned about your ability to deal with new situations?
3. What have you learned about coping with pain?
4. What have you learned about friendships?
5. What have you learned about forgiveness?
6. What have you learned about communication in a relationship?
7. What have you learned about honesty?
8. What have you learned about remarriage?
9. What have you learned about standards and convictions?
10. What have your learned about God?

God, help me to learn as much as I can each day from where I have been.

I suggest that you answer these questions on a separate sheet of paper. You are probably going through some rough times right now, but each answer signifies a learning experience. As you move farther down the road in your growth, you will add more answers to the questions. And as today's scripture says, there is joy ahead, even if what you are going through right now is pretty rough.

A happy heart makes a healthy human

When I was sick as a child my mother would make me take my medicine. It was never pleasant. I wondered for years how something that tasted so awful could ever make me feel good again. Many years later, with all our modern technology, most medicines still taste awful.

A cheerful heart does good like medicine, but a broken spirit makes one sick.
—Proverbs 17:22 TLB

There is a human medicine that makes us feel good, and it doesn't taste bad. It's called happiness, and the relief it brings to all humans is life-saving. I will admit that sometimes it is in short supply, and you have to look hard to find it. For those caught in the emotional wringer of divorce, it may appear that happiness has vanished from the face of the earth. When a friend encourages you to smile or laugh, your immediate feeling might be to punch his lights out. You can wonder long and hard if you will ever be happy again.

I am not suggesting here that you laugh at the things in your divorce that are not funny. I am suggesting that you find ways to experience some happiness as you trudge down the divorce pathway.

I have a few suggestions. First, hang out with upbeat friends who are fun to be with. Stay away from toxic friends who have negative attitudes. Second, do a few fun things every week. Don't stay locked in your room, hoping someone will rescue you. Do what you once enjoyed and attempt some new things that are fun. Third, be good to yourself. Do a few kind things for *you* each week. Kicking yourself through each day just leaves you bruised and bloody. That doesn't make for a happy heart. Finally, realize that God is not against you having some happiness in your life. You don't need to do penance for your divorce and wear black for the next three years.

God, help me to become a happier person and have a cheerful heart.

Remember, happiness is the best medicine for broken spirits!

The tyranny of the shoulds

Many of us carry around a long list of the things we *should* do. Some are healthy and need to be done, while others are unhealthy and only give us an overdose of guilt when we don't follow through on them.

My *should do*s give me a complex, whereas my *can do*s give me a choice. There is a fine line between the two.

The *shoulds* often cause a mental pileup in our minds that can easily lead to physical and emotional decline. *Shoulds* keep us looking backward rather than forward. The *can do*s keep us looking and moving forward with excitement and expectation.

If you were to spend a few minutes right now and list all your *should do*s on one sheet of paper and your *can do*s on another, which list would be longer? From my experience, many people going through divorce spend too much time stewing and brewing over their *shoulds*. They are often prompted by remembering their marriage and contemplating all the things they *should have done* to make the marriage work.

Often, the people closest to us provide us with our *should do* list. If you are not in charge of your life, you will find yourself living out someone else's agenda rather than your own.

God can give you the strength to turn your *shoulds* into options and opportunities for growth. Today's scripture says our strength to live in healthy and positive ways comes from the Lord. When His strength is filling us, our journey in life will become a *can do* adventure.

It is God who arms me with strength, and makes my way perfect.
—*Psalm 18:32*
NKJV

God, release me from the shoulds *I cannot change, and help me change the things I can with Your help.*

Change is the key to the future

He had been married for only a short time when his wife left him. He had been in our workshop for six weeks and seemed to be keeping things together. His parting comment the last night described his recent journey accurately: "The changes in my life are coming so fast, I can't catch all of them."

The wisdom of the prudent is to understand his way.
—Proverbs 14:8 NKJV

To many of us, it appears that changes either happen too fast or too slow. When we are in the valley of pain, slow change is nerve racking and frightening. When our lives are successful and we are moving along in the fast lane, changes are welcomed and keep us moving. We feel successful when the changes are good.

Success and growth in any area of life are based on our ability to accept and process changes. We usually have two basic attitudes toward change. We can accept change or reject change. Our struggle is that we become creatures of habit, and habits, once formed, are hard to change. They become comfortable after a time, and once we reach that comfort level, the need for change can seem unimportant.

Change is seldom a one-way street. It may start with one person deciding to change, but very soon others are affected by those changes and eventually may even be changed themselves.

God, help me to process change in my life and know that You are in control of those changes.

We often try to avoid personal change by thinking it is everyone else, and not us, who needs to change. The problem is we can never make anyone else change. The only option we have is to change ourselves.

Today's scripture is aimed at helping us understand our journey and the changes we need to make in transit. Understanding change is often confusing and difficult. It is the key to your future, and without it, you may be locked out.

So you want to remarry someday?

When questioned about the possibility of remarriage, many divorced people immediately answer, "Never again!" From my experience, those are the first people to remarry.

Now that you are running scared, let me share some practical wisdom with you about a potential remarriage someday in the distant future.

Many second marriages fail because the people preparing for them do little or no preparation. Two of the biggest issues that most men and women need to work on are trust and fear. One is based on the person's past experiences, and the other is based on that person's future. Many marriages, perhaps even yours, ended when trust was violated. When someone you trusted breaks that trust, you may find it very hard to trust anyone ever again. Fear will raise its ugly head and tell you this new person will treat you the same way your former spouse treated you. You may search for guarantees in trust, only to realize there are none because people are subject to change.

Trusting others always starts with trusting yourself. Trusting yourself starts by becoming responsible for yourself. As your personal trust builds within you, you will find it building in others, and some of your fear will dissipate. There is no quick way to go from the darkness of broken trust in your life to the daybreak of new trust. Trust, like everything else, takes time to grow.

It is unfair to immediately place every new person you meet into the same category with your former spouse. There may be a few people out there who are similar to your ex-spouse, but most are not.

Yes, you may remarry someday. Pray for wisdom and healing first.

"Wisdom is better than strength."
—Ecclesiastes 9:16 NIV

God, You know my heart. Help me to renew my trust and not fear everyone.

Too close too soon

It was a simple request. She looked at her group leader and said, "Can I have a hug?" The leader gave her a big hug and tears welled in her eyes. She smiled and said, "Now I feel better." She just needed a loving touch.

Delight yourself in the LORD and he will give you the desires of your heart.
—Psalm 37:4
NIV

In a divorce, human warmth, touch, and intimacy can vanish suddenly, or slowly with every ache of a hurting heart. Many men and women who go through a divorce try to attach themselves too quickly to another person to fill the void. Every human being lives with the need to love and be loved in return. Hurt and rejection only fuel that need and send you looking high and low for an answer. Many single-again men and women become emotional sponges in search of loving saturation.

Over the years, I have listened to countless divorcing and divorced people say they just want someone to touch or hold or hug them, nothing more. That can be an honest declaration of one's humanity if they are willing to stick with the *nothing more* part. Many of these people become susceptible to new physical relationships. A brief encounter may become a permanent relationship, and a second marriage results and individual growth is denied. The road through divorce country is marred by the emotional collisions of men and women who got too close too soon.

God, hold me close and surround me with the warmth of Your presence today.

It is an honest desire to want human closeness and warmth in your life. You want it even more when the pain of divorce burns through your very soul. Today's scripture presents one way to trust God with your needs. If we are satisfied with Him and delight in Him, we can trust Him in His timing to bring the right people for us into our lives.

Be strong and get to work

If divorce is the failure of a relationship between two people, and it leaves scars on both husband and wife, how do you bounce back after a divorce without feeling everything you now do will end in failure? I have heard that question over and over during the past twenty years. Divorce can touch other areas of your life and cause you to live under mountains of doubt. Self-doubt is a step in the wrong direction that can cause other failures.

When we try to reach beyond failure and rebuild our lives, we come face-to-face with real fears:

1. I might fail again.
2. I'll just look stupid if I try again.
3. I might get hurt again.
4. People around me won't like me anymore.
5. I'll lose everything (and I don't have much left).
6. I might lose my job or career.
7. God may be angry with me.
8. Something worse will happen to me.
9. I'll never get rid of my guilt.

That's only a short list. You can add your own fears to it.

Today's scripture is a powerful encouragement to those facing the enormous task of rebuilding their lives. This verse says we are not to be frightened by the job we face, but we are to get to work, knowing the Lord is working with us in every aspect of our life-reconstruction project.

Put out your *Under Construction* sign, and get to work.

"Be strong and courageous and get to work. Don't be frightened by the size of the task, for the Lord my God is with you; he will not forsake you. He will see to it that everything is finished correctly."
—1 Chronicles 28:20 TLB

God, give me Your strength and courage so that I can go to work on my growth and know I will do a good job.

Caring enough to confront

The anger showed on his face when he spoke. His words had the intensity of an electric current: "I'd really like to give her a piece of my mind!" Everyone else in the room seemed to be shaking their heads in agreement. I guess there is always someone we would like to confront, tell off, and give a piece of our minds to.

Confrontation with another human being is hard for most of us. Telling others how we feel and listening to how they feel can be pretty scary. We tend to lose our breath, say things we really don't mean, and get red faced and sweaty in the process. When it's all over, there is often a bigger gap in the relationship than before.

Honesty is a part of confrontation. We wonder how honest we should be and what our honesty will do to the other person. If he or she counters with his or her own honesty, how will we handle it? In confrontation, some things should be faced and spoken, whereas others should be filed away. It takes great wisdom to know what to say and what not to say.

Today's scripture sets the format for any and all confrontations. It tells us to always be truthful and always be loving when we speak that truth. It also says that our goal will be to grow up to maturity in Christ. Instead of giving someone a piece of our minds, if we follow this scripture, we will be giving them a piece of our hearts.

You certainly have to care and love enough to confront anyone. And you need God's help.

But, speaking the truth in love, [we] may grow up in all things into Him who is the head—Christ.
—Ephesians 4:15 NKJV

God, confrontation is hard for me, but when I must confront someone, help me to do it in Your love.

Life at the turning point

Turning points must be action points if they are to help us grow. Living with them means several things. First, it means that you open your life wide to any and all possible changes. You don't live with an arms-folded approach to life. You open your arms wide and learn to embrace the opportunities and possibilities that come your way. You become an adventurer and explorer rather than a settler.

Second, you open your life up to the "no guarantee" way of living. This means you are not afraid of making a wrong decision or going in a wrong direction. You learn that there are no guarantees outside the guarantee of God's love and His promise that He will be with you in every decision and wherever you go.

Third, you become a risk taker. You leave your comfort zone and walk on the water. When someone says, "I wouldn't do that if I were you," you are more determined to try. You quit playing safe all the time and start to live where only your faith and trust in God can get you through.

Fourth, you believe that God is always with you in your experiences. He never sends you out alone. He walks through them with you, one step at a time.

In his book *A Way Through The Wilderness*, Jamie Buckingham says, "There is a day in every life that comes unannounced, unheralded. No trumpets sound, there are no lightning flashes, but as we look back on it, we realize that day was the turning point of our life."

Divorce is one big turning point. Look to God as you make your journey. He will guide you through.

Turn us again to yourself, O God of Hosts. Look down on us in joy and love; only then shall we be saved.
—Psalm 80:7 TLB

God, be present at all my turning points so I don't get the wrong directions.

Give your family a solid foundation

One of the enduring struggles that single parents face is how to build a Christian foundation in his or her family after divorce has splintered the primary family system. A frenetic pace of life often obscures the daily need to have Christ at the center of your single parent family. It becomes increasingly hard to get everyone to eat together a few times a week, let alone pray together or read the Bible together. Sunday can be equally difficult, as each child and adult goes in different directions at church.

Apply your heart to instruction and your ears to words of knowledge.
—Proverbs 23:12 NIV

There are several basic scriptural principles that, if practiced, can give a solid foundation to your home. They are quite simple to read over, somewhat harder to convey, and even harder to live out in a family setting. They are:

1. *Accept one another.* Many children and even some adults don't feel accepted in their families.

2. *Love one another.* It makes every family run more smoothly.

3. *Bear each other's burdens.* This is where love becomes an action word.

4. *Forgive one another.* This keeps the channel of love open.

5. *Serve one another.* Most of us want to be served rather than to serve.

God, these five things are tall orders. Help me to model them and teach them to my family.

You might want to add a few others from your own list. These five are all admonitions from the scriptures. They were proclaimed widely in the early churches because they were the basis of what Christian community was all about. Without them, Christians would be no different than anyone else.

Put the list on your refrigerator door this week and begin to work on it in your family.

Called to be friends

One of our group leaders told me that one of our small groups was still getting together once a month, two years after our workshop ended. He asked if they held the record for staying together the longest. One Sunday a month, they and their families get together for a time of fun, food, and warm fellowship. They say they all feel like a family and plan to stay that way.

It is strange, but true, that we often make our best friends when we are going through our worst crises in life. It may be because our need is great for kindred spirits or that we are most open, honest, and vulnerable in these times.

Our friends form support systems around us. They give us a reason and purpose to live when we feel we have none. Friends are the glue that helps us stick to reality. They keep us in touch with who we really are and where we are really headed.

Author Paula Ripple says, "Without God's love, we cannot discover who we are. Without the love and friendship of human companions we become less than we are. Without faithful companions, we risk not only losing our courage, but even our way."

None of us were intended to be lone rangers. We were planned by God to share our lives in community with others. It means you will have to reach out once in a while to others and allow others to reach out to you. Don't be afraid to try.

"Greater love has no one than this, than to lay down one's life for his friends."
—John 15:13
NKJV

God, I thank You for my friends. Help me to keep my heart open to others who need me as a friend.

Living in the self-control room

Last of all I want to remind you that your strength must come from the Lord's mighty power within you.
—*Ephesians 6:10 TLB*

We were discussing the many ways that our circumstances control us. As the conversation wound down, one of the group members summed up her own feelings and those of the group. She said, "You know what my biggest problem is? I just have no self-control anymore. Everyone else has taken over my life."

Most of us can identify with her comment. Self-control is the toughest control room in the world to operate. At times it's overwhelming. You really want to control your own life, but at the same moment, you wish you could find someone to do it all for you and not make any mistakes.

Some of the self-control areas that divorced people battle with are attitudes, anger, sexuality, physical considerations (appearance, looks, weight), relationships, children, and family. You may want to add a few of your own to this list. Hopefully, you are winning some of these battles of self-control.

Today's scripture speaks about inner strength in the life of a person seeking to follow God. The center of that inner strength is God's power. Real self-control in anyone's life comes from the inside out, not from the outside in. If God is at the center of your life each day, He will supply the strength and power to build your self-control. As one of His children, He certainly doesn't want you out of control or in someone else's control.

You may need to tell God that things in your life right now are out of your control or far beyond your ability to control, and you need His help to regain control. God will give you insight, direction, and wisdom. As you allow God to control you, I believe that your self-control will increase dramatically.

God, I am struggling with self-control in some areas of my life right now. I know the strength I need comes from You. Fill me with Your strength today.

Setting your boundaries

Did you ever meet a person with no boundaries in his or her life? You can identify these people pretty quickly. They usually have someone else's footprints right across their foreheads. They have been without boundaries for so long, that they have allowed other people to walk all over them. They are like a farmer with a herd of cattle, a thousand acres of land, and no fences. Soon the cattle disappear because the boundaries were never set by the farmer.

Boundaries allow us to function smoothly and take care of our own needs so that we don't get walked on by everyone around us. We don't build up walls of resentment and anger when our boundaries are in place. We learn what our limitations are, and we feel free to tell others what they are. It may seem strange, but boundaries give us tremendous freedom and peace. Having no boundaries can give us headaches or ulcers and make us depressed.

Today's scripture is an instruction regarding our boundaries. It forms the spiritual dimension of boundaries and tells us the real blessing will only come when we stay within the boundaries God has set for us in His Word and within the Christian community. If we wander outside God's boundaries, we can get trampled.

Ask yourself today if you have set some healthy boundaries in your life personally and spiritually. If you need to do that, ask for God's help and get started.

Stay always within the boundaries where God's love can reach and bless you.
—Jude 1:21
TLB

Lord, I am not sure that my boundaries are in place. Grant me Your wisdom and guidance to establish healthy ones, both personally and spiritually.

Why me, Lord?

When something wonderful happens to a person, I have never heard that person whine, "Why me, Lord?" Yet, every time something awful happens to a person, I hear that question asked over and over again. I guess what we are trying to say is we deserve to have good things happen to us, but we don't ever deserve any bad things in our life. Christians sometimes think if they try to do everything right and please God, nothing bad should ever happen them. I know many people who ascribe to that kind of errant thinking.

I listen to the Why me, Lord? question in every workshop I teach in the divorce recovery field. I would have to admit that there are many wonderful people going through a divorce. They really haven't done enough bad things to deserve a divorce. So they ask the question and struggle for some kind of answer.

I think today's scripture answers our question. In plain words, it says we are all in the soup together in life. Good people have bad problems, and bad people have bad problems. We all face our realities on the playing field of life. The difference is that the Christian who is seeking to follow God and still has problems knows he or she has Someone to help with those problems. And not just help in some of them, but "in each and every one."

I think I would rather be a Christian with bad problems, knowing that God was going to help me with them, than a non-Christian with bad problems, believing there was no help. It makes a big difference when you know you are on a winning team, even if you are mired in problems up to your neck.

When something good happens, we can truly praise the Lord. When something not-so-good happens, we can still praise the Lord, because God is there to help us.

The good man does not escape all troubles—he has them too. But the Lord helps him in each and every one.
—Psalm 34:19 TLB

God, I thank You for all things today. Thank You for being with me in the midst of my struggles and for helping me through them.

Home is the real testing ground

We have all heard of the man with a thousand faces. He was a master of disguise, and no one knew what he really looked like. Most of the people I know don't have a thousand faces. They usually just have two. One they wear when they are out in public. The other they wear when they are home. Sometimes the two faces look pretty much alike, whereas at other times they are as different as night and day. The real struggle for most of us is to be consistent no matter where we are, at home or outside our home.

For many divorced people, home life often gets strained, frayed, and slightly torn. Agendas, needs, and feelings all congeal together to steal away some of the quality of home life. Many single parents over the years have said they feel they no longer have a real home, just a house where people eat, sleep, and come in when the weather is bad.

Today's scripture talks about a quality of life that honors God and will be a blessing to all the members of the home. I believe it sets the parents out front as leaders in that home. Children were never called to lead their parents, but parents were called to lead their children.

It is hard to be a role model for your family when all your energy goes to just surviving your divorce and making ends meet economically. Weariness and always running behind can cause you to forget God has called you to be the captain of the ship called *Home*.

Home is the place where we most often reveal our true selves, and it is the place where we need the most help from God. Stop long enough each day to ask for His help in your home.

I will try to walk a blameless path, but how I need your help, especially in my own home, where I long to act as I should.
—Psalm 101:2 TLB

God, I do need Your help in my home. My heart is strong, but my body and spirit get weary. Give me Your strength each day.

The gift of perseverance

The legalities of divorce can test your patience to the maximum. Legal work takes long stretches of time in which very little appears to be happening. No matter how often you call your lawyer, nothing seems to move any faster. Most divorcing people know one thing: They want their divorce finalized so that they can get on with their lives.

Waiting for things over which you have no control takes great patience. Keeping your life moving while you are waiting takes strong perseverance. I meet many people in the divorce process who want to take any shortcut they can to get out of the legal freeze they are stuck in.

Today's verse has nothing whatsoever to do with how slow things are going legally in your divorce. It has everything to do with your faith in God to always keep things moving and growing in your life. No matter what piles up, with God's help, you keep moving one step at a time. The scripture says that when God does His part and you do your part, you will be filled with the joy of the Lord. And that joy will take away any impatience you might have over anything.

Some of us have great perseverance, some of us have little. Some keep moving ahead, and some stop moving altogether. Some possess the joy of the Lord, others are devoid of it. One thing is for certain. We can ask God for what we need and know that He will supply it. And we can ask our friends to pray for us.

We are praying, too, that you will be filled with his mighty, glorious strength so that you can keep going no matter what happens—always full of the joy of the Lord.
—Colossians 1:11 TLB

God, I feel like quitting about twenty times a day. Help me to know Your strength so that no matter what happens, I will trust You and stand firm.

Welcome to the weak

Each time he said, "No. But I am with you; that is all you need. My power shows up best in weak people."
—2 Corinthians 12:9 TLB

When I asked him how things were going, I was stunned by his response. "Getting weaker by the moment," was his reply. I thought he had the flu or a cold or some other miserable discomfort. But what he had was a messy divorce, which was slowly sapping his energy and threatened to render him immobile. You can be a tiger in everything you do in life and end up drained and weak from a divorce.

Many men and women in our divorce support groups tell me they come each week for an injection of hope and wish they could stay in their group all week long. They feel strong when they are with other group members and weak when they are all alone.

In the moments when you have to be alone and cannot be with other supportive friends, it is important to know that God is with you. Today's scripture affirms that fact and pointedly tells you that His being with you is all you need. Don't get nervous. This doesn't mean it's just you and God and nobody else. It means that God is your anchor of stability. The latter part of today's verse defines how God helps us in our tough places. His power comes through best when we have absolutely none. His power invites us to allow Him to give us the strength we need when we are getting weaker by the moment.

God, I thank You that You are with me today. May Your power sustain me today in my weakness.

Our weakness is an opportunity for God to come alongside us and give us His strength to meet our challenges. You can trust Him today to do that. When your strength is renewed, you will know it came from God. When you have His guarantee, the rest of your journey will be easier. His signpost to us is *Welcome to the Weak.*

Getting even is expensive

It sat in her driveway with four flat tires. They were not flat hours ago when she went out with friends. As she approached the car, she noticed that all four tires had been slashed. And she had a pretty good idea who had done the slashing. Her former spouse had told her she would be sorry if she left him. A few days later she told me she had devised several ways to get back at her ex-spouse, and she would extract her own vengeance. Revenge is all too common in the ongoing battle of the Ex's. Some vengeful acts even end up in the death of a former spouse. That happens everywhere in America. It happened to a friend of mine some years ago.

Getting even can be expensive in many ways. It takes its toll on us physically, emotionally, financially, and spiritually. It robs us of energy we could put to better use. It causes us to live life on the defensive and to wonder what will happen next. The game of revenge can go on for years, and it is often played out through the children. In the end, no one ever wins and everyone loses.

God's way of handling things is often not our way. The scripture says if someone hits you, turn the other cheek. If someone hurts you, love the person in return. We really don't want to hear these things. Today's scripture tells us not only to do no evil things, but also not to even think about them. Now that is really difficult.

Don't think about revenge and don't take revenge. Get on with the more important stuff in your life like doing the laundry and washing your car.

To plan evil is as wrong as doing it.
—Proverbs 24:8
TLB

God, I confess to You that I would like to get revenge sometimes. Help me to release those thoughts to You and focus on rebuilding my life.

Gifts for your children

About two million children in America every year are affected by the divorce of their parents. Most lose a parent from their home, many lose their home, and all of them wonder what else they may lose in the divorce process. The following Bill of Rights for Children of Divorce was put together by our staff. I share it with you today in hope that you will share it with your children and let them know you love them and that they still have some rights left in their lives.

And now a word to you parents. Don't keep on scolding and nagging your children, making them angry and resentful. Rather, bring them up with the loving discipline the Lord himself approves, with suggestions and godly advice.
—Ephesians 6:4
TLB

Children of Divorce Bill of Rights

1. The Right to know that I am loved unconditionally.
2. The Right to know I didn't cause my parents' divorce.
3. The Right to know what caused the divorce.
4. The Right to the security of where I will live and who I will live with.
5. The Right to be aware of how stress affects my life and how I can adapt to it in a healthy way.
6. The Right to be a kid and not to be afraid of being myself.
7. The Right to have the guarantee that my physical and emotional needs will be met.
8. The Right not to be a victim of the past marriage and not to be used as a pawn between my parents.
9. The Right to have my own space for privacy to · ensure respect of my person.
10. The Right to have a normal household routine and discipline to warrant a sense of security.
11. The Right to possess positive images of my parents so that I can love each parent equally.
12. The Right to have access and time with each parent equally.

God, thank You for my children. Help me to reach out to them with a right spirit and great doses of love.

When criticism counts

When was the last time you thanked someone for the criticism he or she directed at you? Probably a long time ago, if ever. Most of us have a difficult time with any form of criticism. We usually interpret it as a attack on our integrity or behavior. When it is aimed at us, we immediately throw up a wall of self-defense and start our rebuttal, or we retreat into a place of safety and silence.

Don't refuse to accept criticism; get all the help you can.
—Proverbs 23:12 TLB

There are two kinds of criticism. You have probably heard both of them in your journey through divorce. They are constructive criticism and destructive criticism.

Constructive criticism is usually applied gently and with a strong sense of affirmation. It is designed to help a person improve and become better in a given area. It does not attack the person but is directed toward the problem. It gives a person a chance to respond and make changes. It is intended to be in the best interest of everyone.

Destructive criticism is directed toward the person rather than the problem. It dehumanizes and gives the person no place to stand. It is often a judgment and shows no mercy. It often ends up with a character assassination.

Today's scripture may sound funny because it tells us to be open to criticism because it will help us. We know it has to be the right kind of criticism though if it is to be of any benefit. We have to learn to listen with an open heart and mind when someone criticizes us. Because we know God speaks through other people, it may well be the way God is trying to help us make improvements in our lives.

God, when I have a critical spirit, touch me with Your love. Help me to accept the criticism that will make me a better person and reject the kind that tears me down.

Remember, constructive criticism builds people up whereas destructive criticism tears people down. Remember that we are to speak the truth in love. If you will always be careful to apply that word in giving and receiving criticism, you will get real help and know you are loved along with it.

Inching closer to God

You may have seen the bumper sticker that reads, *If you are not close to God, guess who moved?* That slogan tells a lot about our relationship with God on a day-to-day basis.

Come close to God and he will come close to you.
—James 4
JBP

I meet many people who expect God to do all the moving and all the work, as well. They want to be close to God and have a healthy relationship with Him, but they expect to stand idly by and let God put forth all the effort. In case you haven't heard, God doesn't work that way.

Any human relationship that is to grow must start with two people investing an equal amount of time with each other. If one person lets down in the relationship, it will lose intimacy and strength. The same is true in our relationship with God. In today's scripture, James puts a strong emphasis on our responsibility to direct our relationship to God by moving toward Him. As we do that, the distance between us and God is diminished, and a growing closeness can be established.

How does a person draw closer to God? There are several ways. We are closer to God when we spend time talking and listening to Him in prayer. We draw closer to God when we spend time reading, studying, and meditating on His Word, the Bible. We also draw closer to God when we spend time with other members of God's family in worship and fellowship.

God, I want to draw closer to You. Help me to deepen my relationship with You each day.

A crisis such as divorce can either draw you closer to God or drive you away from God. I have seen it do both. Some want to blame God for their divorce and run away from Him. Others know they need God's help and start to pursue Him and deepen their relationship with Him. Are you inching closer to God today?

Big trouble calls for a big God

You are in big trouble! There probably are no words more fear inducing than these spoken by a parent to a child. As parents, we use these words at moments of total exasperation. We never build up to that statement by first saying, "You are in *small* trouble." There is no easing into the big arena of trouble. It is a quantum leap from no trouble to big trouble. When you are in big trouble, you are going to have big problems.

I will call to you whenever trouble strikes, and you will help me.
—Psalm 86:7
TLB

When you are an adult and you are going through a divorce, no one needs to tell you that you are in big trouble. You usually tell yourself and everyone around you just nods in agreement. Within a few short weeks, big trouble often turns into *life threatening trouble,* and you know you are going to need help.

We begin to resolve trouble with one word: *Help!* That help can come in two ways: from people who love you and care about you and from God, who also loves and cares about you. But you have to do the asking.

A certain humility of spirit will allow us to ask other humans for the help we need. A strong arm of faith and trust will allow us to reach out to God and ask Him for help. Today's scripture is both a declaration of need and a promise of help. When you need help, you must initiate the call for help and then believe that it is God's desire to help you. You must also know that you can ask God for help as many times as you need it. God will always be there for you, even if you feel that you might have worn out your plea.

God, help me today to give You all my troubles and know that You will help me.

Big trouble in your life calls for a big God. The God we serve is big enough to rule a mighty universe, yet small enough to live in our hearts. You can call on Him right now.

Putting God first

As I write these words it is the first day of a new month. It means I pay my bills, stand in a very long line at the bank, turn to a new month on my calendar, and put appointments for this month on my daily agenda. Life is made up of a succession of "firsts" on all our calendars.

Set your heart first on his kingdom and his goodness, and all these things will come to you as a matter of course.
—Matthew 6:33 JBP

My pastor, Dan Yeary, recently talked about the five ways God wants to be first in our lives. His points are well worth sharing. Some may be new to you, while others you know and practice already.

1. God wants the first part of every day you live. He wants to meet you personally before you meet anyone else.
2. God wants the first day of every week. This we know to be Sunday, and God wants us to be present in His house to worship Him.
3. God wants first place in all our personal relationships.
4. God wants us to give Him the first dime of every dollar we make.
5. God wants us to give Him first consideration in all our decisions.

That's a pretty good list for your life and mine. Today's scripture tells us that if we put God first, all the other things that we place so much emphasis on will be taken care of by God without our worrying, sweating, or fretting.

God, I think I get my priorities messed up from time to time. Help me to put You first in all things and know You will take care of everything.

It is hard to even think of first things when we are struggling to stay afloat in a divorce crisis. If we choose to put God first in the right things, however, the matters of divorce will be taken care of by God, and we need not worry about them any longer.

First things first is a great motto. God's things first is a better motto.

Morning talk

Some people wake up talking in the morning, while others don't say an intelligent word until noon. Some hit the floor running when they wake up, while others can't even find the floor. For all of us no matter how we welcome the new day, morning symbolizes a fresh start and new opportunities. Heavy clouds of memories that hung over us in the night seem more distant and less ominous at daybreak.

My voice You shall hear in the morning, O LORD; in the morning I will direct it to You, and I will look up.
—Psalm 5:3 NKJV

I believe it is important to meet God in the morning before the day's agenda and priorities take possession of you. It may mean getting up thirty minutes earlier and getting to bed thirty minutes earlier. If meeting with God is haphazard for you now, it will take serious discipline to reform your mornings. You will not succeed without a struggle.

The psalmist encourages us today to lift our voices to God in the morning and look up to Him. Our voices can be employed through prayer, praise, singing, or reading scripture out loud. Our intentions are to renew our line of communication with God and place Him at the starting gate for our new day. When we leave our home and move into the day's activities, we go knowing that He goes with us.

As we start our day with God, I believe we can also close it with Him. In monastic communities around the world, every day starts and ends with a chapel time for the monks. The day is opened with God and closed with Him. And when you are on monastery grounds, you will quickly sense a peace and calm that I believe is the result of those moments with God. You quickly get a sense that God is in charge here, and His presence is not just a Sunday thing.

God, I want to hear Your voice the first thing every morning, and I will work at Your hearing my voice the first thing each morning.

How is your morning talk time with God going? Is it time to set some new priorities and meet God at the beginning of each new day?

The relational roller coaster: part one

"**I**'m too old, too tired, and too broke to play this date, relate, and mate game. Is there another way to find that special person for my life?" I have heard that statement and question a thousand times. When a divorce is finally over and you begin to realize there is a life beyond it, the first question that often comes up is how to build healthy new human relationships. You may not want to remarry for a very long time, but you don't want to live in a state of relational deprivation either. There are some real keys to becoming responsible and accessible in relationships as a single-again man or woman.

1. Look at every new person you meet as a potential friend. It takes time to build a friendship. You seldom do it with one encounter.
2. Build friendships with members of both sexes. Men need women just as friends, and women need men just as friends.
3. Avoid using relationships just to fill the holes in your life. Remember, things are for using, people are for loving.
4. Realize that most of the relationships we make in life are temporary. We receive from people, we give to people, and we allow people to pass on through our lives.
5. Watch out for relational messiahs. They want to rescue you, but there is usually a price tag attached to their help. Relational messiahs are dangerous people.

Today's scripture (and tomorrow's) tells us we belong to God's family. Our best new relationships will be with other members of that family. If we view them through that lens, we will be more loving, kind, and gentle with them.

Consequently, you are no longer foreigners and aliens, but fellow citizens with God's people and members of God's household.
—Ephesians 2:19 NIV

God, building new relationships is hard. Help me to focus on friendship as my goal and not fear.

The relational roller coaster: part two

What if I get hurt again in a relationship? How can I avoid that? I have listened to those questions in counseling and in seminars for the past twenty years. And I have learned that there is no guarantee against one person or the other getting hurt. Pain is a part of most relationships because people are human and can cause pain.

As a guideline for healthy relationships today, here are five more suggestions (continued from yesterday).

6. Don't believe that a sexual relationship outside the context of marriage has a money-back or money-in-the-bank guarantee. Some singles use a sexual encounter to hang on to a relationship, while others use it to gratify their own needs.

7. Take time to shape up and make yourself attractive. It can be hard work, but you're worth it.

8. Look at all friendships as an opportunity for the giving and receiving of gifts. Some of those gifts are trust, affirmation, availability, confidence, love, accountability, and encouragement.

9. Learn to become an interesting person to others. How many of your friends would you classify as interesting? Are you one of their interesting friends?

10. Spend time building some brother-sister relationships. Treat those relationships with respect and love.

Life and the building of solid relationships can often seem like a roller coaster ride. There are highs and lows, and twists and turns on the ride. The ride is sometimes scary, but it's also a lot of fun. You certainly don't want to take it alone!

Consequently, you are no longer foreigners and aliens, but fellow citizens with God's people and members of God's household.
—Ephesians 2:19 NIV

God, help me to add more healthy relationships to my life. Thank You for making me a part of Your family and for giving me countless brothers and sisters.

The parenting just goes on and on

She looked dog tired. It had been one long week of working, running errands, taking care of two sick kids, helping one get started in college, and getting the other two off to camp. As we talked, she said, "If I would have known I was going to be divorced, I don't think I would have had five children. I wonder who will still be living when the last one is on her own?"

She probably summed up the words of many single parents across America. There was no relief in sight, and her parenting would just keep going on and on. She loved her children. She just wondered if she had the endurance to complete the child-raising process.

Parenting does not end after a divorce. It just gets more complex and more frenetic. There are split schedules, shared parenting, and if a former spouse remarries, there is a whole other family to deal with. Jealousy often runs rampant in post-divorce parenting.

In previous pages you have read how the Lord has promised to meet all your needs and take care of you. Now your question may be, "Who helps care for my children?"

Today's verse is a promise for your children. You need to know it, and they need to know it. Perhaps the word *forsake* is rather harsh here, but in some ways, lots of children have been forsaken by their parents. When that happens, God moves in and expresses His care and love. You can really thank God for that today!

When my father and my mother forsake me, then the LORD will take care of me.
—Psalm 27:10 NKJV

God, I thank You for loving and caring for my children. Help me to teach them of Your love.

Moving on with my children: part one

He had just spoiled Sunday dinner by asking his children the worst question they could ever imagine: "How would you all feel if we moved back to the East Coast?" He told me an uproar followed his question, and the shock waves it sent out lasted for the next week.

Children have their support systems just as adults do. Moving is one big destroyer of those systems. Adults don't like it, and children like it even less. Moving at the end of one's junior year in high school is the trauma of the century for any teenager.

From years of working with the children of divorce, I have some "moving on" wisdom to pass along to you today and tomorrow. This wisdom comes in nine guidelines that we have shared in workshops around the country.

1. Weigh carefully where you and your children will live in the post-divorce years. This is important whether you are the custodial or the noncustodial parent. Children need to be involved in this decision.
2. Make ongoing financial support for your children a priority in the post-divorce years. They need to understand this.
3. Remember special events in the lives of your children. Noncustodial parents often find this difficult, as they are not physically present in the children's daily lives. There is little worse than forgetting a child's birthday or meaningful events.
4. Remember the importance of touch. It is easy to get consumed with your own needs and forget those of your children. Touch is vital to the emotional well-being of your children.

The next five guidelines are in the devotion that follows. How are you doing with the first four?

I have set the LORD always before me; because He is at my right hand I shall not be moved.
—Psalm 16:8
NKJV

God, help me to remember to make my children a part of all my decisions.

228

Moving on with my children: part two

If you have children still living with you after a divorce, they will affect any decisions you will make. I have watched some parents decide to move on and not worry what their children thought. It doesn't take long for the children to feel uncared for when that happens and start initiating their own form of rebellion.

Here are the last five guidelines for moving on with your children.

I have set the LORD always before me; because He is at my right hand I shall not be moved.
—Psalm 16:8
NKJV

5. Surround yourself with memories of your past for both you and your children. Too many parents rid themselves of the past by trashing all their memorabilia. Your children have a right to those archives.
6. Give the gift of time to your children. Do special things with them to let them know they are vital and important to you. They don't need to be big things.
7. Make your children a priority and let them know they are. As a single parent, you may find that hard time-wise. But work at it each day.
8. Be aware of the role changes after divorce. Your role has gone from team parenting to single parenting. When you begin to date, roles can change again. When you remarry, a gigantic role change comes into both your life and the lives of your children.
9. Remember that your children will always be reminders of your former spouse. Physical characteristics are only a part of that. Personality traits also are inherited.

God, being a parent beyond divorce is hard work. I know I can do it with Your help.

Your children deserve a healthy and growing relationship with both parents in the years after divorce. You deserve the same with them. It will take work on both sides. God is at your right hand to help. Just reach out to Him.

The gain from the pain

I say the words in every divorce recovery workshop. I've been saying them for the past twenty years. *There is no gain without pain.* Everyone usually moans when I say it. They all know it is true in every area of life.

"Do not sorrow, for the joy of the LORD is your strength."
—Nehemiah 8:10
NKJV

Much of the pain in divorce is caused by unhappy memories of the experiences people had to live through. Some have said they really need a good dose of memory healing so that they can move on with their lives. Unhealed memories can prevent growth and cause years of misery.

In a book by the Linn brothers called *Healing Life's Hurts,* the authors suggest a process of healing painful memories. There are five progressive steps that people walk through.

1. I won't admit that I was ever hurt by anything: *Denial*
2. I blame others for hurting and destroying me: *Anger*
3. I set up conditions to be fulfilled before I'm ready to forgive: *Bargaining*
4. I blame myself for letting hurt and pain destroy me: *Depression*
5. I look forward to growth and gain from my hurt and pain: *Acceptance*

God, I am not ready to thank You for my pain just yet. I am ready to begin my journey into healing and wholeness with Your help.

You can think about this a little and decide where you are today in your struggle to grow from the pain you have been through in your life. All healing in any area is a process and will take some time. If you are unwilling to commit to the healing journey, you may be in pain for a long time to come.

In all we attempt to process, the Lord is still our strength. You can hold on to that scripture today as you walk through the valley of pain to growth!

Welcome back

A divorce can drive you away from God or it can draw you to God. I have watched it do both many times in people's lives. The happy part for me is seeing people drawn to God because they know they cannot survive their situation without God's help and seeing how God works in their lives to give them strength, courage, and new hope.

I meet some people going through a divorce who once were close to God but lost that closeness for one reason or another. The crisis of divorce often beckons them back to the family of God. Some have even told me they felt as though they were finally home again after many years of living life on their own terms, only to discover they were a long way from anything God had for their lives.

Today's scripture is a reminder that God is in the business of showing kindness and mercy to all who return to Him. The scriptural reference is to Israel's persistent wandering from God. There was always a leader, a prophet, or a king telling Israel to get back to God and reminding what God had promised if it would return to Him. For a while Israel would get it right, then off it would wander again pursuing its own pathway.

You and I are a lot like Israel. We get good directions and are full of good intentions and off we go following God. Then we get distracted with other things and sail off course. Boom! A crisis hits, and we are jarred back into reality and know we need God's help. We are fortunate that God is patient with us, or we would be lost in deep weeds.

God established a forgiveness pattern long ago. It is still in operation today. If you have been gone from God for too long, are you ready to return to Him? His kindness and mercy are there for the taking. He will welcome you back!

"For if you turn to the Lord again, your brothers and your children will be treated mercifully by their captors, and they will be able to return to this land. For the Lord your God is full of kindness and mercy and will not continue to turn away his face from you if you return to him."
—2 Chronicles 30:9 TLB

God, thank You for Your patience with me. I want to draw closer to you. Help me.

231

Moving forward in relationships

The Lord is my light and my salvation; whom shall I fear?
—Psalm 27:1 TLB

They were both talking excitedly as they approached me at the end of the seminar. They thanked me for the six weeks we had spent together, and then one of them said, "Do you know what the best thing in this workshop was for me?" "What's that?" I asked. Her reply was to reach out and hug her new friend and say, "Mary!" Then they both smiled at me and walked out into the night.

The best gift some people get in a workshop is a new friend. Few come expecting that gift. Most come looking for answers and identification.

On a previous page, I mentioned that after a divorce, a person can lose 75 to 80 percent of the friends he or she had when married. This can leave a gigantic relational void in your life when you are in a place where you need the support and encouragement of all the friends you can get.

Friends are lost and won in the tough places of life. Don't spend too much time wondering about those who have drifted away. Put your energies into building a new support system. Most of your new friends will probably be divorced or divorcing. Their level of compassion and understanding will be far greater than that of people who are still married.

Spend time looking for a healthy single adult group that you can join. Find some friends in that group who have moved down the road and grown through their divorce. Spend time with people who can energize and motivate you. Stay away from people who moan and groan and never get beyond their divorce. Plan to do fun things as well as growth things with your new supportive community. Look for relational activities that are challenging and will get you out of your cocoon.

We all have two choices in friendships. We can spend time with nourishing and positive-thinking friends, or we can spend time with toxic or negative-thinking friends. As you look at relationships, think about who needs to exit your life and who needs to enter.

God, help me to move forward with new relationships in my life today.

Moving forward in personal goals

Name one personal goal that you have set for yourself that is not contingent on anyone else. Do you have one? Are you working toward it with excitement and expectancy?

For many men and women going through divorce, personal goals are either way down on their lists or are nonexistent. Any major life crisis has a tendency to crush past goals and send you the negative message that goals are a waste of time. Some people say that they had a goal of staying married, and because that goal went in the dumper, there is no point in setting any further goals.

Without a few personal goals that you can take ownership of, life can become pretty aimless and empty.

Here is a simple formula that I read somewhere about setting personal goals. As you think and dream about two or three personal goals, use this list to record your process.

1. Be specific in your goals. Generalizing never gets much accomplished.
2. Find a way to measure your progress. Goals must be measurable.
3. Goals must be attainable. If they are not attainable, call them dreams.
4. Goals must be result-oriented. This is a measuring device. It is also a form of reward.
5. Goals must be time bounded. No deadline, no finished product.

A vital part of moving forward through your divorce is to have personal goals you are working on each day, each week, each month, and each year. When you reach any goal, big or small, have a celebration. You deserve to reward yourself for work well done!

Nevertheless, the righteous will hold to their ways, and those with clean hands will grow stronger.
—Job 17:9
NIV

God, help me set a few personal goals for my life and seek Your help in attaining them.

Moving forward in vocational goals

They are on the freeway in our city every weekday morning. Commuters going to work. They are back on the freeway in the evening returning home. I always wonder how many are excited to get to their jobs in the morning and how many are sad to leave in the evening. How many people really love their vocations? How many people hate their jobs and only serve time there each week?

Does your vocation cause you more happiness than unhappiness? What is the emotional reward for what you do to make a living? What would be your vocation if you could do anything you wanted? What would be the price tag to doing that?

When anyone is hit by a life crisis, such as divorce, everything should come under the review microscope as you think about moving on and rebuilding your life. Vocation is just one item on the list.

I have met many people who have changed vocations completely after their divorce. I meet others who stay in the same job track they have been in for years and are completely happy.

There are no vocational guarantees anymore in our society. Occupations become quickly outdated. Companies downsize or merge. Technology changes overnight. Uncertainties abound in our vocational world, but options and opportunities increase.

You may be living the occupational dream of your parents or family. It may be time to review the dream and compare it to what you feel in your heart.

Resources abound today to help you review your career and help you plan for some of the rest of your life. There are always pros and cons connected to career change or career enhancement. Is it time for you to move forward in setting some new vocational goals?

But they that wait upon the Lord shall renew their strength. They shall mount up with wings like eagles; they shall run and not be weary; they shall walk and not faint.
—Isaiah 40:31
TLB

God, help me wrestle with this question about vocation and not be weary. Guide my future.

Moving forward in educational goals

It arrived in Sunday's paper. It was the local community college catalog for the new school year. It was crammed with every imaginable course, subject, and topic under the sun. When school opens in a few weeks, all the classes will be at capacity as people of all ages register for courses. Community colleges were once the domain of high school graduates who either needed to improve their grades before going to a four-year college or for graduates who didn't have the funds to go to a four-year college. Not so today. Over half the student body on many community colleges is well beyond the age of thirty and contains adults going back to school to either change a career or find one. Some are there because their companies sent them for additional training in a specified field.

As you move forward through your divorce and begin to rebuild your life, do you need to take a second look at furthering your education or returning to college to finish a degree? Many of the people in our seminars today are going to school full or part time. Some have set some long-term educational goals and are working at them one course at a time. I know it is a slow process, but the end result makes the trip well worth taking.

A person five years beyond his divorce put something into perspective for me the other day. He said he had two lives, one prior to divorce and one after divorce. He added that his goal was to be educated in his second life. You may share his feeling. It all starts by getting a college or university catalog. Visiting the registrar's office and obtaining some funding comes next, followed by setting a starting date for your first class.

God will walk with you through the halls of academia and give you wisdom and strength for the journey.

God is alive! Praise him who is the great rock of protection.
—Psalm 18:46 TLB

God, is it time for me to go back to school? Lead me, guide me, and let me know what You want me to do.

Moving forward in family goals

Keeping a strong sense of family after a divorce is not an easy task. Divorce has a tendency to divide family members rather than pull them together. Fathers and mothers often fight for allegiance from the children and use them as weapons to get back at the other parent. Children get lost in the shuffle and relate better to their peers than their parents.

But as for me and my family, we will serve the Lord.
—Joshua 24:15
TLB

Family doesn't end with divorce, but it does take on a very different form. It takes a strong commitment for a custodial parent to make family a priority for all its members. It may take more commitment for the noncustodial parent to keep the sense of family alive and vital.

Moving forward in setting family goals beyond divorce involves asking and answering three tough questions. Both parents and all the children need to do it.

1. What is most important in our family right now?
2. What gives our family meaning and purpose?
3. What do you want to be and do in the life of your family?

To those general questions, I can add three more that have a spiritual impact for the divorced family's future.

1. What is the most important spiritual goal for our family?
2. How can our family deepen its walk with God?
3. What is God trying to teach and say to our family?

God, help our family to set some goals that will draw us even closer to each other in the days ahead.

You can add your own as you think about moving forward in family goals with your post-divorce family. Remember to emphasize the fact to all members of your family that *We are still a family!* Even if some members are on their own and now have their own families. Families are forever!

Moving forward in health goals

He sat in the workshop each week alternately shaking and dozing off. When I finally spoke to him and asked how he was doing, he said, "I'm an emotional and physical mess. Otherwise I'm doing fine." He later told me he could not eat or sleep much and was taking several different tranquilizers. In brief, he was a physical wreck and getting worse by the day.

Divorce affects the physical and mental well-being of many people. Some overeat whereas others starve. Some drink and others pop pills. Some sleep all the time and others can't get any sleep. You know you are in a battle for physical survival but aren't quite sure how to fight the enemy. And the battle can go on for months.

Moving forward in setting some good health goals is important to your survival and personal growth. I have told numerous people that a good starting goal involves having a total physical, learning to eat well, and getting a good physical workout each day. Add enough sleep and some good vitamins, and you are at least in the starting gate for your marathon run through and beyond divorce. Too many men and women going through a divorce just don't care enough about themselves to work on maintaining good health. If it doesn't become a daily discipline, it will be hit and miss.

You have a responsibility to take care of yourself physically. That may mean dieting to lose added pounds, joining the YMCA or a local health club, riding a bike, or walking or jogging. There are many ways to get a program going that works in your life. Your body is God's temple, and treating it well brings glory to God.

For you were bought at a price; therefore glorify God in your body and in your spirit, which are God's.
—1 Corinthians 6:20 NKJV

God, I need to get some goals for physical health. Guide me Lord, and give me a gentle shove in the right direction.

Moving forward financially

The newspaper said her divorce settlement was a million dollar home, a high priced foreign automobile, and $28,000 per month. And she wasn't even a movie star or a famous person. She lives here in my town and apparently is going to live far better than most divorced people I meet. She is a long way from the poverty line financially.

Divorces wreck family finances and get very expensive if contested. They still cost a lot many months after the divorce is finalized. Many men and women struggle for years after a divorce to become economically stable again.

Moving forward financially after a divorce involves learning to handle your finances, even if you never handled them before. It may mean getting help in forming a budget and paying bills. It may mean learning how to get out of an economic mess or bankruptcy. The good news is that competent help is available everywhere today. Your church, bank, financial institution, and community college can all assist you. Your part is assessing where you now are financially and deciding where you would like to be down the road. Knowing where you are is half the battle. Getting to where you want to be is the other half.

A woman in a recent seminar was ecstatic as she told everyone she had just bought her first house, in her name and with her money. Everyone cheered and applauded because after her divorce she had been left with a mountain of bills. She took a big shovel and started digging herself out. Now, several years later, she had achieved her goal.

It is important to be content where you are, as today's scripture indicates. But the good news is you don't have to stay where you are. You can move ahead by working hard, getting good advice, and trusting God with all you have.

Not that I speak in regard to need, for I have learned in whatever state I am, to be content.
—Philippians 4:11 NKJV

God, help me set some financial goals for my future. Thank You for meeting my needs today.

Moving forward emotionally

Mad, Sad, Glad, and Scared. The science of psychology says these are the four most basic of all human emotions. At any given time of our waking day, we might find ourselves experiencing one of them. To tell someone where we are emotionally is risky. They might accept the way we feel, or they might not. It is difficult to know just when we can be authentic emotionally or when we need to say nothing and move on.

The experience of divorce can dump a river of emotions on you and leave you wondering how to prevent being drowned in them. There are two ways to deal with those emotions. You can repress them, smile at everyone, and say you are fine all the time. That's called lying if you know you are not fine. Second, you can find trusted friends to express your emotions to and allow them to be a buffer for you. They are not responsible to change them, solve them, or deny that you have them. They are responsible to hear you out and receive them from you. We all need to be heard because it authenticates our existence. Not being heard says no one cares.

As you move forward emotionally, you process your feelings and, I hope, unload some of them. If you are still mad ten years from now, you have been dragging your garbage with you. There is a time to put emotions and feelings behind you and move on. Growth is an opportunity to know yourself, be yourself, and express yourself.

We can act on our emotions and feelings, or we can react to them and let them dominate and own us. We always have choices. Have you moved forward emotionally and worked at putting your feelings in a healthy perspective? If not, ask God to help you begin to do that today.

"You didn't choose me! I chose you! I appointed you to go and produce lovely fruit always, so that no matter what you ask for from the Father, using my name, he will give it to you."
—John 15:16
TLB

God, some days I'm overwhelmed by my feelings. Help me process them in a healthy way.

Moving forward spiritually

If someone stopped you going into your church next Sunday and asked you how you are doing spiritually, what would you say in response? Fine? None of your business? Terrible? Don't ask? I think most of us would smile and say we were doing fine. Is it really anyone's business how we are doing spiritually? Yes, it is God's business and should be the concern of a few of our spiritual friends.

In the spiritual realm, we are either growing spiritually or we are not. If not, how can we get back on track and get our lives moving again?

Moving forward spiritually means I should be way ahead of where I was last year at this time. I should even be farther ahead next year at this time. If that is to happen, I must formulate a spiritual growth plan for my life and learn to stick to it. That plan should include the following: a daily time for prayer; a daily time to read God's Word; a time for silence and solitude each day; a time for scriptural meditation; a time to read Christian literature; a time to write briefly in a spiritual journal; a time for worship with other Christians; and a time for sharing with spiritual friends.

Those are just a few of the basic ingredients to help you move forward spiritually each day. You should also ask yourself where you want to be spiritually one year from now. In what areas do you need to grow spiritually? If you don't plan to grow and grow a plan, you will be the same a year down the road as you are today.

Today's verse presents a wonderful idea—"living in his presence every day of my life." That is a goal that daily disciplines can enhance. What one thing would you ask God for today to help you move forward spiritually?

The one thing I want from God, the thing I seek most of all, is the privilege of meditating in his Temple, living in his presence every day of my life, delighting in his incomparable perfections and glory.
—Psalm 27:4
TLB

God, I want to walk with You each day. Help me be more disciplined.

Moving forward by listening to others

God uses other people in all of our lives. The truths that they echo in writings or in person add to our growth. Many of those truths stick with us all of our lives. In times of struggle, we repeat them over and over and draw strength from them. Next to scripture, the truths spoken by the people in our lives are probably the most powerful things God uses to touch us. Here are a few of my favorites that may touch you in a special way today.

Seek the Lord while you can find him. Call upon him now while he is near.
—Isaiah 55:6
TLB

"Living in gentleness is making room for the voice of the Divine in our lives." —Adrian Van Kaam

"God is bigger than our blunders and not immobilized by our sins." —William Hulme

"Humility is walking in the truth of who we are." —St. Teresa of Avila

"I am not afraid of my life." —Susan Muto

"You only know what victory is when you have been part of the battle." —Henri Nouwen

"Faith never falls apart at the approach of the boulders in life. It is when the rocks are rolling that faith shows up best." —Malcolm Smith

"The wind of God is always blowing but you must hoist the sail." —Francis Fenelon

"If you want to grow in openness to God, you ought to seek the company of God's friends."
—Thomas Green

God, thank You for speaking through Your servants to my heart. May these words and Your words touch my spirit today.

These are words of wisdom, and you might want to post them on your refrigerator door and read them daily.

If you want to travel, don't take a guilt trip

"I should have been able to prevent this divorce. If only I would have tried harder, this wouldn't have happened." When was the last time you echoed those words? I hear them several times a week from men and women who have been ambushed by their inability to change a situation called divorce. The longer they repeat those lines, the deeper they fall into the guilt trap. Once you are buried in your guilt, you become a prime candidate for depression.

For if our heart condemns us, God is greater than our heart, and knows all things.
—1 John 3:20 NKJV

There are two kinds of guilt: positive guilt and negative guilt. Positive guilt keeps you from repeating the same mistakes over and over. If we feel guilty about overeating to the point of feeling sick, that guilt should keep us from overeating to that degree again. Negative guilt is feeling guilty about things we had no control over. All the guilt feelings in the world will not change something that has already happened. You can always learn from your experiences, but negative guilt is a poor teaching tool.

I don't know too many people who have not taken a few guilt showers during their divorce experience. The most common guilt here is feeling guilty over what your children must go through and continue to live with after a divorce. Some children can add to your guilt by telling you the divorce was all your fault.

God, remove the guilt I drag with me each day. Thank You for being greater than all my guilt.

Today's scripture speaks to the feelings we carry in our hearts. Many divorced men and women carry a heart full of guilt. It is important to know that God is greater than our heavy heart and that He fully understands how we feel. This is why the scriptures tell us many times over to give our problems and concerns to God because He can resolve what we cannot.

It is not God's desire to have His children buried under mounds of guilt. His forgiveness for what we feel we have done wrong can remove our guilt and set us free to live in His love.

Keep the love coming

I have been told that restoration is a painstaking process. I admire those who restore old cars, old furniture, old houses, and old lives. Attention must be given to detail and the work must progress slowly. There is no instant restoration process. Those of us who like things done instantly wonder how anyone could have that kind of patience and love for a project.

Restoring love from the remains of a broken marriage takes time, patience, and a large amount of healing. Divorce is love gone wrong, love abused, and love abandoned. What once was abundant and promised to be everlasting is now dissolved.

It is hard to begin receiving and giving love when you are unsure that it even exists anymore. It is even harder to tell someone that you love them for fear they might abuse that love and plunge you back into the valley of rejection.

There are three areas to work on when you are learning to love again. First, your love for God has to grow and become stronger, or if it has disappeared, it must be reborn. Second, you have to love yourself. That may be even harder than loving God. If your self-esteem has been crushed, the return to self-love may be very slow. Third, you have to reach out again and start loving those around you, even if they do not show love to you in return. That's risky because there are no guarantees in loving.

The love restoration project after divorce is one of the most needful things you can work on. It is time consuming and often painful. But you will grow from it. Start today, and keep the love coming.

Continue to love each other with true brotherly love.
—Hebrews 13:1 TLB

God, I think my love has dried up since my divorce. Help me to restore love to every area of my life.

And finally, may God grant you peace!

Congratulations! You have reached the final page of *Moving Forward.* I hope you did not just jump from page one to this one. If you have spent your time reading a page a day, you should now understand a few things. First, God still loves you even if you are divorced. Second, God still has a plan for your life and a future for you. Third, it's a long and winding road to recovery from a divorce. Fourth, you are not alone, and God can bring a support group around you to aid in your recovery process.

You and I will probably only know each other through these pages. If we could talk one to one, I would want to assure you that no matter where you are today, there is life for you beyond divorce. In twenty years of working in the field of divorce recovery, I have watched thousands of men and women come through divorce with God's help and emerge on the other side to new life and growth. You will too.

What is my prayer for you today after all these pages? I pray that you will have a peace in your life now that can only come as a gift from God. I know as you do, that peace is a rare commodity when you are going through divorce. Divorce for most people is chaotic, much like a war. It is only on the far side of that war zone that you will experience a new peace in your life. God is the Author of that peace.

Today's verse tells us to pursue peace with everyone— even our enemies. That's the human part. The other pursuit is to seek holiness. That's the God part. When we combine the two, the promise is that we will see God. I believe that is worth working for in your life and mine.

May you be at peace with those around you today, and may that peace come from God.

Pursue peace with all people, and holiness, without which no one will see the Lord.
—Hebrews 12:14
NKJV

God, surround me with Your peace and teach me to walk holy before You! **Shalom!**

About the Author

Jim Smoke is a well-known speaker and author of nine books, including the best seller, *Growing Through Divorce*. He is founder of the Center for Divorce Recovery in Tempe, Arizona and serves as adjunct professor at Fuller Seminary in Pasadena, California.